KALI RISING

Foundational Principles of Tantra for a Transforming Planet

RUDOLPH BALLENTINE

TANTRIKSTER
PRESS

Cover design by Aleksandra Jelic
Cover art by Ed Rihacek
Illustrations by Lotus Grenier

Printed in USA on recycled paper

ISBN   0-578-06954-7
EAN-13   978-0-578-06954-8

Tantrikster Press
PO Box 392
Ballentine, SC 29002

*This humble work I offer at the lotus feet of
my beloved master Shri Swami Rama of the Himalayas
Whose infinite love and patience is the foundation
for all that I have done and will do.*

Acknowledgements

I want to thank all the women in my life who have brought Her voice through clearly and inspired me, especially Pennell, Rebecca, Helen and many of the women in the community where I live. Of course I owe immense gratitude to my teachers, especially Swami Rama, who so patiently imbued me with the principles discussed herein. I also want to thank Pundits Rajmani Tigunait and Mark Dyzchowski for their kind help and support, and Susana and Galen, who read the manuscript first, and reassured me of its value.

Many thanks to my old and dear friend, Ed Rihacek, who generously offered the beautiful cover work, to Lotus Grenier, whose bold drawings grace the pages inside, and to Aleksandra Jelic for the tasteful design.

Additional thanks to Linda Bark for always being there, and for shepherding this book into print, and to all my tantra trainees who co-created this work with me over many years of courageous and growthful play together.

TABLE OF CONTENTS

ORIENTATION

Why Tantra? And Why Now?

A s I sit to write this in 2010, few would disagree that the world has
entered a period of dramatic change. Many would go so far as to say
that what is taking shape is an upheaval of epochal proportions. In any
case, change is in the air. And it is not change limited to one sphere of human
activity. Rather, it seems to be across the board.

I am both alarmed by, and enthusiastic about, this change. Much of my preoccupation with it is probably the result of my training and career. I worked for
nearly forty years as a holistic physician. Before that, I completed a residency
in psychiatry (during the wild sixties in New Orleans where I co-founded a
"free clinic" in the French Quarter and tended idealistic young hippies on bad
trips). Over those many decades, my turf was the transformative crisis that led
to healing and to a heightened consciousness. I feel something similar coming
toward us now.

What we face

The impending re-gearing that we are entering now is awe-inspiring for its
depth and breadth. This reshaping of our world is evident on many fronts.
Certainly there is economic change. Many fortunes are being lost, a few made,
and entire countries are seeing their balance sheets crumble. The environment
is reeling even more drastically: temperatures changing, waters rising, storms
and earthquakes increasing in frequency and/or severity. Our foundation in
nature is being shaken.

Meanwhile, closer to home, we find other of our customary refuges in a state of disruption. Traditional family structures continue to deteriorate. The familiar gender roles of prior generations are called ever more into question. The core relationship between husband and wife, for example, is riddled with doubts and uncertainties. What is the proper role for a woman, a mother? A man, father? Or does it even make sense to ask anymore what is "proper?" If not, then exactly how does one proceed to establish a relationship? Or even more pressing, a home for children? What seemed like freedom, begins to feel like confusion and chaos. Is it really possible to reinvent everything all at once?

And the upheaval is not only in the world around us. There are corresponding baffling challenges in our inner world – e.g., basic issues of identity: who *am* I anyhow? As nationalities merge and morph, ethnic groupings are less and less clear and their importance more and more doubtful. Facing all this – this tidal wave of change – our own sense of what is natural and spontaneous begins to feel shaky.

And that takes its toll on our health. Immune systems flag and fail since the very essence of immune function is to defend a clearly identified entity. As identity becomes blurrier and more uncertain, immune function wobbles and wanes. How do I know what to eat if I'm not all that sure who I am? Moreover, we are discovering that in general our habit has been to abuse, not just to use, our bodies – all those habits need to be rethought, too. Without those familiar habits, our sense of self is further eroded.

Meanwhile, our spiritual life, our connection to some inner presence greater than ourselves, is also often jarred loose as we grapple with all the changes that we are experiencing within and without. While some try to recapture the simple precepts of the past, for many others the familiar landscape of religion, with its comfortable assumptions and assurances, seems curiously remote from the wrenching changes that we are caught up in.

How are we to respond to all these pressures we are subject to? Though we each have our own ways of coping, most of all, for most of us, there is a felt need to be able to grasp in some overarching fashion what is happening, to see the larger picture, to find a framework broad enough to reveal how these many shifts might reflect some common dynamic. Unfortunately, our western reductionistic mindset, so well suited to analysis, falls short when it comes to a synthesis such as this. What's needed is a kind of thinking that is integrative, holistic – or, even more than that, *holographic* [*].

[*] See Glossary page 213 for information on such terms.

Looking East for Help

This is where the wisdom of the East serves us better. It provides us with a way of proceeding that is not restricted to the linear, not given to reflexive analysis —a way of thinking that is larger of scope, friendlier to the synthetic, unruffled by contradictions that exist on the level of mechanistic logic. An openness to the possibility that something can be both true and not true is what has come to be called "fuzzy logic," and it is the harnessing of this peculiarity of Eastern thought that is said to have enabled Japanese engineers to create a train that glides so silently by at such breathtaking speeds, while our western equivalents clickety-clack along with their ancient Newtonian designs.

While the perspectives of the East are generally more hospitable to the kind of grokking that we need to do now, what is of particular interest is that there are sub-currents in the stream of Eastern philosophy and spirituality that are more specifically of value to us in our present dilemma. For example, Taoism in China, and Tantra in India are movements that separated themselves from the mainstream of their cultures so as to cultivate and nurture a more radical probing of the nature of humanity and its relationship to spirit. Often regarded as potentially too disruptive to the prevailing social order, they were relegated to the periphery of society, and generally given wide berth. Similar sects and renegade groups were accommodated in various analogous ways by many cultures, and have existed in dynamic dialectic with the mainstream, challenging and revitalizing the dominant culture repeatedly [*].

The contribution of such radical subcultures has been enormous, and they are particularly valuable at times of major upheaval and transformation. This is because they are capable of making sense of things at a time when the familiar order is unraveling and its perspectives no longer feel valid. They are unafraid of the apparent chaos of change; it is their element. In fact, the very purpose and *modus operandi* of these radical subcultures is to study and develop the science of *transformation*. Their traditions and teachings are commonly encoded in disciplines such as Alchemy, where they are often subject to disdain an arrangement that is convenient for both the mainstream—which wants to modulate the input from the counterculture—and the radical movements themselves—which must be concerned about the sanctity and freedom of their ongoing experimentation and explorations.

But now there seems to be a growing willingness – a thirst, even – to take a deep drink at the spring of such transformative wisdom. Perhaps we know that

[*]   See Annotated Bibliography: Prem Saran, *Yoga, Bhoga, and Ardharnarishwara.*

chaotic reconfiguration is upon us, and are eager to learn the secrets of how this works and how to stand steady in the storm – perhaps even how to delight in the process.

And an example of what we find—a new paradigm strategy leaning heavily on the transformative traditions of the past – is to look for the holographic dynamic. I.e., what is the transformative commonality in all these crises – climate, economy, social order, gender morphing, health collapse, spiritual and religious soul searching? Just as a fragment of the holograph reveals the outlines of the entire picture—though not with the sharpness you get when you see the whole—what does each crisis, looked at in depth, suggest about the gestalt?

What this book will suggest is that each piece of the puzzle, each specific crisis we find ourselves confronting currently, reflects this common core dynamic: a chronic indifference to the needs of our embodiment, i.e., our physical bodies, the Earth, the community of humans – in other words, the matrix which sustains us – and a denial that it is that *matrix* that is also the source of our life force, our creativity, our power. The book shows how attempts to find power elsewhere have failed, and have led only to the pervasiveness of a sort of "faux power" which is (whether subtle or blatant) essentially *violent*.

The other facet of this recurrent, pervasive dynamic (and another theme of the book) is that the collective force of the thwarted life force is gathering now, and is readying itself to push forward and through all obstacles to reassert its primacy.

The book represents this gathering storm by the traditional Indic image of Kali, the creator/destroyer – She who rises to reassert the supreme power of the creative (more precisely, the *feminine*) principle.

That image, a central one in the tradition of Tantra, illustrates the intent of this book: to mine the savvy of the radical countercultural sages of the world to help steady and ground us as we enter the storm of transformation that seems to be approaching. Thus will we fortify ourselves with a multidimensional vision that better enables us to discern the emerging patterns of change as they coalesce, flower, and bear us along toward the as-yet-unforeseeable future.

Why Tantra?

Though the language and concepts of this book are tantric, there are many traditions – Eastern and others, that also deal cogently with transformation. Tantra however, is unique in several ways that make it especially suitable for the task at hand.

First, it has survived relatively intact in its richness and detail for well over a thousand years. Many other of the relevant ancient traditions are available to us now only in partial form.

Second, Tantra has served as a sort of (counter) cultural crossroads, receiving input from sources as varied as tribal shamanistic practices throughout South Asia to the lofty philosophies of Kashmiri Shaivists, as well as from a spectrum of major world religions, including Buddhism, Hinduism, Sufism (Islam), and even Christianity and Judaism [*], and (in the Himalayas) Taoism.

Third, Tantra paints itself on a huge canvas: It deals with the relation of the human with the Infinite. Yet, at the same time, it is eminently practical. It is always keeping one eye on the nitty-gritty of embodiment: the earthy issues of sex, survival, and power – as they manifest in the world of instinct, emotion, and bodily fluids and functions. And it has the intention of integrating them in such a way that they are spontaneous and uninhibited, yet aligned with the highest expressions of spirituality as well.

Fourth, Tantra is perhaps unique in the emphasis it places on the relationship between Masculine and Feminine, its perception of the pervasiveness of that dynamic and how it runs through human to divine, from heaven to earth, and from microcosm to macrocosm [**].

And last but not least, Tantra is explicit in how it places all this in the context of our collective transformation, the eminence of our planetary transition into a new, already emerging consciousness (which we will call "the Integral" [***]). Tantra views this (at least on the microcosmic level) as a movement from the consciousness of the superficial intellect to the more profound consciousness of the Sixth Chakra.[****]

[*]   Most notably in South India.
[**]   Tantra's appreciation of the central role of Masculine and Feminine may be due to its openness to exploring all the aspects of sexuality as well as its embodied (experiential) study of the bilateral (right and left) nature of breath (ida and pingala) and mind (right/left brain dichotomy).
[***]   See glossary.
[****] Located in the vicinity of the pineal gland, the so-called "Third Eye," whose nature is a deeper "seeing".

Such a description of its distinctive features suggests that Tantra offers perspectives and insights that are missing from Western thought [*]. Before detailing some of those, I would like to provide a brief summary of my own struggle to comprehend the profundity of Tantra and to articulate it for the contemporary (especially Western) mind.

But Which Tantra?

If you have read many of the multitude of current books on the subject of Tantra, you are probably aware that there are "many Tantras." Not all of them reflect the descriptors sketched out above. As we shall see throughout the course of the book, Tantra is built around authentic self-expression. It follows that to some extent each person will need to create her or his own version of it.

My own version, what I share with you, is a product of my experience as physican and psychiatrist, as well as my twenty-year preceptorship with my teacher, Shri Swami Rama of the Himalayas. It is also colored by my study and teaching in the field of sacred sexuality, and my longstanding concern about current socio-economic and environmental issues. A few more details might help put this in context.

After I completed medical school, an internship, and a residency in psychiatry, my path, by the early seventies, was leading me from the ferment of the New Orleans counterculture to the ashrams of India, where I met Swami Rama. With his guidance, I began to carve out a model of Holistic Medicine that integrated yoga, ayurveda, homeopathy, and a fistful of other modalities that enhanced self-awareness and personal transformation. For us, illness was only a bump in the road of personal and spiritual unfoldment, and when the process of transformation was supported (through yoga, meditation, homeopathy, etc.), disease most often faded away.

The insights gained from those decades of work I summarized in the book *Radical Healing* (which is woven around the principles of Tantra). Soon thereafter, with nearly forty years of practice behind me, I resigned, turning my attention to teaching what I saw as the backbone of that work: the science of transformation as articulated in the theory and practice of Tantra.

[*] In fact, until recently some of these perspectives and insights probably could not have been integrated into Western thought. It is only in the last fifty years, perhaps as a result with increased cultural contact with Eastern thought, that the concepts, vocabulary, and awareness necessary to make this possible have been acquired by Western writers and teachers.

That my teacher was teaching us Tantra was not something that he stated explicitly. The challenges and pitfalls of teaching embodiment [*] – especially when they veered into the realm of the erotic – were not topics easily tolerated in the America of the 1970's and 80's. It was only after I had completed a twenty-year mentorship with him and turned to my own unexplored inner frontiers, that I discovered that what I had learned from him was most accurately termed "Tantra."

Therefore, as I began in the late 1990's to teach the tradition I had assimilated over those decades, I struggled to formulate what had been conveyed to me in a way that would represent it accurately to other westerners. In so doing I drew also on my training in psychiatry, my knowledge of medicine and healing, and found myself immersed in a contemporary meeting of East and West.

While Swami Rama had taught us key Upanishads and other such classics of Indian philosophy, there was much to go back and fill in. And much of all this, though rich and profound, was, I realized, largely inaccessible to those who had not spent twenty years in the world of Indic culture. So I cast about for writings by Westerners who had stumbled upon the similar truths. Though much of this literature lacks the coherence and simplicity of the Eastern versions, it is stated in terms more familiar to our Western minds, and often provides at least a entrée into what is otherwise off-putting. Much of what I present in this book is such an amalgam of East and West, ancient and modern, using the more accessible Western as a bridge into the more concise and well-integrated Eastern. And much is a product of my own personal journey, and those of my patients and students.

Some of the concepts and insights that come from the East during such a process of cross-fertilization, fill spaces in the Western world view that had felt "empty" and wanting to me. For example, Tantra assumes, and constantly implies, that we exist and function on more than one level – in more than one reality. While Western thought is beginning to acknowledge that there may in fact be other dimensions of existence, Western science generally disregards the data that indicate such non-material realms of being, so mostly these phenomena live in the group awareness only as dream, myth, or science fiction.

---

[*] *Embodiment* here is intended to indicate a goal of those philosophic and spiritual traditions that aim to bring their teachings into integration with the instinctual – with sexuality, emotions, and issues of domination and submission – in such a way that they are trustworthy spontaneous expressions of Spirit, rather than impulses that must be suppressed or disowned in order to live the precepts of the tradition.

This severely limits what Western inquiry can approach. It certainly makes any cogent treatment of a subject like Tantra very difficult, since the majority of what it is about must be ignored. The work of Jean Gebser (1905-1973), European philosopher and academician, is of immense value here. In a Herculean feat of integration, he assembled the most respected and sophisticated contributions of Western thinkers to demonstrate that their collective work strongly implies a spectrum of what he called "structures of consciousness" that we "inhabit." Besides our everyday waking consciousness, there is, for example, that which corresponds to the dream state (which we in the West largely maintain as separate from waking consciousness). Another, even deeper and even less often conscious, has to do with the awareness of such phenomena as subtle energy. Gebser's work lifts us out of our psychological parochialism, i.e., out of our assumption that the way we have constructed our inner world is the only way it can be done, and makes clear that the mixing and mingling of these types of consciousness varies dramatically from time to time and from culture to culture. This perspective and the language that he provides for such a new discourse enable us to begin to put into (these newly expanded) Western terms a fuller treatment of such previously baffling subjects such as Tantra.

A second missing piece that tantra supplies is that shakti, or creative energy, is the foundation and essence of power and that it arises from a distinct "fountain" within the human, what Tantra calls the Feminine, and that this is different from its counterpart, the source of consciousness, termed the Masculine. In other words power is an attribute of the Feminine in *each person.* (There is no "masculine power;" men access power from their Feminine.) Attempting to "make things happen," to "rule," without coming from that inner source of creative energy (which is the Feminine) can result only in brutality, abuse, and the crushing of creativity in others.

A third point is that pleasure and play are the essence of spirituality. It is only when we are in touch with our spontaneous delight that we access the collective unfoldment of planetary evolution. As we shall see, the whole world view of Tantra is valuable and it must be grasped to some extent as intact in order to appreciate it fully. Nevertheless, the above points are particularly valuable to the West.

While the attempt to integrate critical aspects of Tantric thought into our Western conversation and to adapt and make it understandable runs through much of the book, probably the most obvious of the innovations I have made is in how to talk about the different facets of the Masculine and the Feminine. Though the different aspects of the Masculine and Feminine are clearly present for South Asians as the varying faces of the gods and goddesses, this is not so for westerners and non-Indic peoples. So I have adopted the distinctions proposed by Genia Pauli Haddon in her ground breaking book Uniting Sex, Self, and Spirit. As a Jungian, she is grounded in the idea that each person, male or female, is, in her or his inner world, both masculine and feminine. But in her book she goes a step further. She turns to the anatomical and physiologic characteristics of male and female as reference points to distinguish between two versions of the Feminine (Yin and Yang) and the two versions of the Masculine (Yin and Yang) [*]. This allows us all to recognize and honor the assertive Feminine (what Haddon calls the Yang Feminine) and access the *power* that it offers [**]. This aspect of the Feminine has been virtually erased from our cultural awareness. (See Appendix C for more explanation of the Haddon terminology).

Another elaboration of traditional tantra is the identification of the violence of the current version of the Masculine. This, the book proposes, arises from the impotent rage of a culturally distorted Masculine which, in turn, is a result of his alienation from his inner Feminine, the (only) source of genuine *power*. Though it would seem that this is essentially a western phenomenon (at least in its current exaggerated form) it appears to be becoming more global as the world has become more "westernized".

[*]   At the outset, this may be confusing, since the purpose of her work is to demonstrate the Jungian point that both men and women have a contrasexual – the other gender – represented and operating in their psyches. That the Masculine has both phallic (yang=penetrative) and testicular (yin=containing) aspects is as true for the Masculine of a woman, as it is for the Masculine of a man. It happens that a man (largely because of his hormones) has the physiological support to manifest the phallus and testes rather than the uterus (with its two modes, both yin = receptive and nurturing, and yang = birthing). Though complex, all this is much less confusing for all of us now than it would have been a generation ago, in part because of our experience with trans folk, who regularly demonstrate the mutability of gender and even of the body itself.

[**] More accurately: that it *is*.

ABOUT THE FORMAT OF THIS BOOK

The book consists of two parts: a dialogue, and a commentary. This is the traditional form in which such teachings were passed down.

PART I, is titled **The Kali** [*] **Tantra**. It is in the form of a dialogue between Shiva and Shakti, the primal archetypes of tantric lore. He is the Light of Consciousness, She is the Power of Creation. He explains, i.e., puts into conceptual terms, what She has manifested, bringing the light of understanding to the abundance She has brought forth into being ("birthed").

But that is only a small part of what these two figures mean in Tantra. Their significance is vast, stretching holographically [**] across all levels of existence, from the microcosmic inner world to the macrocosmic workings of the Universe.

On the personal level, they represent the two basic aspects of self and their interaction is seen as the fundamental dynamic of our inner being. We experience this dynamic as the tension and the dance between the right and left hemispheres of the brain, or the right and left *nadis* (energy channels) that run through the body. This inner dance shapes our outer relationships, which mirror the inner one, nudging us toward "living out" the core dynamic of the inner [***].

Beyond the personal, the Shiva/Shakti dynamic is mirrored and replicated throughout the larger world around us. The relationship between these two fundamental aspects of our being, which have almost universally been thought of as masculine and feminine principles, is considered the core dynamic—the dance of the proton with the electron, the rotation of the earth with the sun – the foundational building block of the universe. It is the balance of their attraction and repulsion, the resulting vibration to and fro, that underlies the phenomenon of life itself.

So Shiva and Shakti are our own inner connection with the cosmic. The subtleties of their interactions inform our lives and shape the heavens. To tune into them and to read the complexities of their relationship unlocks the secrets of life.

[*]   The more formal transliteration is Kaalii, which emphasizes the long ah and ee.
[**]   Each specific re-enactment of the Shiva/Shakti interaction being another glimpse of the whole, only with varying degrees of "blurriness."
[***] This is usually most obvious in an interaction between male and female, but, as we shall see, the Masculine/Feminine dynamic also plays out in a somewhat more complex and nuanced fashion within relationships between members of the same sex.

Or at least so taught the men and women who have been the custodians of the tantric tradition. Our exploration in this book is to see if this key to understanding will help us untangle our current confusions, and address the pressing challenges of our changing world.

PART II of the book is a commentary. Using the principles laid out during the dialogue of Part I, it explores how the principles of Tantra might be used to understand what is happening in the world today. There is a chapter each on health, relationships, the environment, the socio/political/economic scene, and the realm of spirituality.

The backbone of this discussion is the uncovering of the hidden violence in our world and how it masquerades as "power," and the discovery that its antithesis—the underlying, anchoring feature of Tantra as an evolutionary discipline—is play. As detailed in this second part of the book, closely related to play is (true) power and pleasure. The three of them together make possible a totally and radically different view of our world and its challenges, and comprise the foundation of Tantra as a spiritual path.

ABOUT THE MEDITATIONS...
Between Parts I and II is a lengthy guided meditation intended to bring the abstract concepts of Part I to life by helping you uncover your own inner Shiva and Shakti. That should provide you a more personal context for the discussions in Part II. For those already familiar with meditation and grounded in a practice of it, this He/She Meditation should be easily accessible. For others, I have offered a series of "meditation building blocks" or "Foundational Meditations" at the end of each section of Part I. If you need further support to be able to settle into the meditation, there is more in Appendix B, The Meditations and Tantra, beginning on   209.

....AND THE TITLE
The title of the book, *Kali Rising*, takes its cue from the birthing energy emergent now on Planet Earth. But just how will it emerge? The most dramatic scenario might feature Kali, with Her awesome, transformative power, sweeping away our paltry civilization, to make room for the arrival of something new. Or, it could, on the other hand, imply that Kali Power is beginning to rise in *each* of us, that returning Her to Her rightful place as the creative force that directs each individual life, and that that, happening in millions or billions of individual humans, will collectively add up to the global change that is required on the planet. Perhaps which of these two ways She rises will depend on how open each of us is to the inner process, and how consciously we nurture and cultivate it.

A KALI TANTRA

An Explication of Fundamental Principles of Tantra for Today

~ by Lord Shiva for his Divine Consort, Shakti ~

PART I

Introduction

Traditionally a *tantra*, which is a writing passed down describing the principles and practice of the discipline (also called *Tantra*), has most commonly been offered in the form of a dialogue between Shiva and Shakti. Shiva is the archetypal embodiment of the masculine principle, often thought of as a descending column of light – the light of consciousness. Shakti is the ascending flame or spark that arises from the earth – the energy that creates life. She is the archetypal embodiment of the feminine principle. As the dialogue opens, She, feeling compassion for the suffering of humankind, approaches Him and asks Him to elucidate the reasons for this painful state of affairs. In the conversation that follows, Shiva, illuminates the process of life on earth, bringing it into conscious awareness, and details how things have gone awry. Shakti, already complete in Her power (with, as far as creating and manifesting, no need or lack), accepts the elucidation grateful for the help that it will offer to embodied souls, all the while basking in its implications, since it ultimately amounts to adoration of Her.

In bringing the ancient principles to a new, more global audience, and allowing their articulation to be shaped to the present and its challenges, such a traditional format seems a natural choice.

How (and why) to read the dialogue

On one level the dialogue here (and in the traditional texts) is an explanation of the basic principles of Tantra. Of course, that could have been done in a more straightforward way. But to recreate the immediacy and the intimacy of a one-on-one conversation brings the teachings to life.

Still that is only the surface of why a dialogue is valuable. Much of what is being conveyed is transmitted through the quality of the interaction of the parties. Of course Shiva and Shakti could be simply described with the hope that you could grasp their nature and the richness and subtleties of how their microcosmic/macrocosmic dynamic works, but how much more efficiently informative to *hear* them interact!

Therefore their conversation should not be regarded as trivial – even (or especially) the apparently off-handed remarks, teasing, and banter. It is a depiction of who they are and the intricacies of how they interact – not only within us but also in the functioning of the world around us. Remember, to the tantrika their dynamic is the key to understanding the nature of the Universe.

Bringing this Shiva/Shakti dynamic into consciousness becomes even more critical when we put it in the context of the current challenges we face on the planet – the multiplicity of psychological, relational, social/political/economic, and spiritual crises that surround us. Let us, at least for the moment, throw in our lot with the tantrikas, and go with their perspective: that a troubled dynamic between Shiva and Shakti is the thread that winds through the major disturbances of the day. Then we will want to probe inside ourselves to look at the relationship between our own inner Masculine and Feminine, which is most often found to reflect that in the world outside and is, as a result, tense and troubled.

Much of what is problematic about the relationship between our own Masculine and Feminine arises from their distortions. These twisted versions of the Masculine and Feminine that most of us find within come from an acculturation that has, over millennia, drifted away from the ideal that Shiva and Shakti might once have effortlessly exemplified.

But, distortions notwithstanding, we work with our own inner Masculine/Feminine dynamic because it's our leverage, our microcosmic input into the macrocosm, our contribution to the "morphic field" [*] that can reshape our world.

[*] See Rupert Sheldrake, *A New Science of Life* (now out in a revised and expanded edition entitled: *Morphic Resonance, The Nature of Formative Causation*).

First we must bring it into consciousness, then it can shift. Listening to their conversation is a big step in this direction.

A Contemporary Shiva and Shakti

As we listen for the voices of Shiva and Shakti, we will most likely hear something a bit different from what was heard a thousand years ago. Certain differences between, on the one hand, our current notions of gender, the Feminine, the Masculine, and the relationship between them and, on the other hand, the corresponding notions of the ancient tradition will become evident.

So, unlike the classical dignified exchanges (mostly Shiva calmly explaining and Shakti serenely listening, apparently confident in Her position as goddess adored), our version of Shiva and Shakti – at least as they appear in this dialogue – will have their moments of contention (even indignation or conflict) as they try to communicate fully. Since our protagonists are found to be fraught with the distortions of the pure cosmic principles of Masculine and Feminine that characterize the current planetary culture on Earth, they struggle at times (as do we) to untangle simple verities from the contaminating conditioning that prevails even in the deepest recesses of the collective psyche.

The dialogue – part of the process of peeling away the cultural distortions that afflict Her and Him – may offend some who will feel it a sacrilege to attribute to Shiva and Shaki human confusions. But there is ample precedence for it. Indic mythology is run through with tales of jealousy, egoism, etc. on the part of the gods and goddesses. Moreover, we are following here the notion of gods and goddesses as archetypes that exist in the realm of the Dream consciousness or *Taijasa* [*]. They are not personifications of the unitary consciousness [**]. Nor, as is stipulated later in the book, does this dream consciousness correspond to the Freudian notion of dream as mere day residue and unconscious projection. Instead, it is meant to indicate the reality that precedes and gives rise to what might be called "everyday waking consciousness." From this point of view, those archetypal shapers of our world also are, over long periods of time and with continual input, themselves reshaped. Thus will our own Shiva and Shakti have suffered such distortion and we will need to "uncover" their true essence through our own individual inner work and our collective cultural conversations.

---

[*] For those unfamiliar with such terms, please use the glossary at the back of the book.
[**] Though in some traditions Shiva is elevated to such role.

In fact, it was probably always so. While Shiva is elevated to position of "the greatest God" in some traditions, in others he takes his place as part of a pantheon – at least alongside Vishnu and Brahma. In many of the countless stories about him, he shows varying human characteristics. He is malleable and mutable – as are all the archetypal figures that shape our world and ourselves. In the words of Mark Dyzchowski, renown Sanskrit scholar and author of *The Doctrine of Vibration*,

> "*Morphing deities and polarities reflect the heave and flow of the Whole Reality of all things. If we lose sight of thatwe have lost the thread that connects us to one another because we are not just individuals, male and female, but epitomes of the one reality spontaneously engaged in the play of diversification and re-integration. The downward and upward movements of this flow reflect the dynamics of inner turning into outer and their perpetual reversal into one another. This is the way the Ancients have taught that the One replenishes itself even as it becomes all things.*"[*]

Much of the distortion of our own internal masculine and feminine aspects may be peculiar to our own western psyches. But despite our differences from the Indic cultures that gave rise to Tantra – the fundamental work of Tantra remains what it traditionally was: making possible the coming to union of the Masculine and Feminine in order to birth the new consciousness. So ultimately we have not really strayed from the traditional tantric schema, we have merely adapted it to changing circumstance.

If a major feature of that tantric work is to birth a new consciousness, its methodology automatically leads to that. By the very act of writing and reading the dialogue, a sort of mediating narrator is implied, a "third I" – beyond the "I am Her" and "I am Him." In fact, as the book will explain (or, better, as Shiva will clarify), this Third I actually corresponds to the "Third Eye" (forgive the pun) or Sixth Chakra. One of the priceless messages of Tantra for us today is that we, the human race, are on the brink of moving into a new and radically different consciousness that we can scarcely begin to imagine – one that will involve a mass activation of the Sixth Chakra. That chakra, which is centered at (and behind) the point between the eyebrows, and involves the functioning of the pineal gland (physiologically a light perceiving organ), has for eons been marked – with the *bindu* in India and in various similar ways in different cultures – to indicate its crucial role on the spiritual path and perhaps, its emerging role in our next human metamorphosis.

So the third personage (hovering implicitly) in this little dialogue will be, not

[*]   Personal communication, 2009.

merely a neutral party, but a harbinger of things to come, a glimpse of the consciousness each of us will ultimately hold as the marriage of Shiva and Shakti
is consummated and a new integral awareness dawns. It is a consciousness that
sees them both, and holds constant awareness of the precarious and, at the
same time, delightful dance that constitutes their ever-morphing interplay.
Meanwhile, this Third I, this *melded* consciousness (assumed by both reader
and writer) has some very practical work to do – Sh/He (It has no gender) will,
as you move through the book, "hold the space" for the dialogue, and begin
to embody the consciousness that results when Shiva and Shakti unite/marry.

Moreover this "Third I/Third Eye" consciousness – that of the reader/observer
– can usefully be taken as a preliminary model for the mediating role of your
own Third I/Third Eye consciousness as you do the Masculine/Feminine
Meditation (described on page 97) |*| which is an important adjunct to the
reading of this book.

|*| There are other, preparatory meditations provided intermittently throughout Part I of the book and
a more in depth discussion of the Meditations in Appendix B

*All honor to Lord Shiva and to His Divine Consort
and Mother of the Worlds, Shakti.*

Feeling the agony of humankind and all embodied life on planet Earth, Shakti, out of infinite love and compassion, approaches her Divine consort, Shiva, and asks him to bring to bear the descending light of consciousness in order to elucidate and unravel the knots of unknowing that lie at the root of humanity's agony.

PRINCIPLES 1 & 2

as elucidated by Lord Shiva for his Divine Consort, Shakti

Principle 1. *Everything is an experiment*

Shiva: The first, and in some ways, the most fundamental principle of our discipline is that everything is an experiment.

Shakti: What do you mean by that?

Shiva: I mean that whatever is done is done with consciousness, so that through the doing of it we learn something. It is, fundamentally, a scientific process.

Shakti: Scientific? That seems odd. I mean isn't science something invented recently?

Shiva: Not really. Maybe the word is new, but the principle is age-old. To try something, and gather the evidence that results is pretty much how intelligent living always proceeded.

Shakti: Well, when you put it that way, I can easily agree, but then it doesn't sound like you're saying much of anything at all. What's the point of that being a "principle" of Tantra?

Shiva: The point is, if you take the experiment idea seriously, then you pay more attention to the process and take more careful note of the results.

Shakti: I can see that....

Shiva: Otherwise, lots of times people do experiments and don't gather the data. The result is they don't learn anything, and they stagnate.

Shakti: So you're actually kind of riding on the general infatuation with the idea of "science?" I think I've heard it said that in current times "Science" has become the new religion.

Shiva: True....The problem there is when people start treating it as a religion, they also usually lose sight of the gathering of evidence and learning part of it...

But the true spirit of science, the curiosity, the desire to find out what is true, the reliance on clear observation and solid data, are all part of the foundation of Tantra. Maybe Tantra can help clean up science – which has, as you imply, gotten sort of sloppy. But in any case, the attitude that goes with the experimental approach is basic in Tantra.

Another reason this merits the status of a principle of Tantra is its assertion that *everything* is an experiment. That means an authentic tantric approach maintains that attitude all the time: the testing, finding out, and learning continues even when you are emotional or when you might be responding to something in a habitual and unconscious way. You've got to be on your toes and not go to sleep if you are really constantly experimenting.

Shakti: Yes, that makes sense. I mean, I get the point, I think, but it still isn't something that thrills me. Is it really that....that *heady*?

Shiva: Well, it is logical...nothing wrong with that...but...It's not merely cerebral, not dry and boring, even though it might sound like it. Definitely there is in the tantric kind of experimentation a light-heartedness, a sense of playfulness....

Shakti: I still feel like I'm missing something here....this dialogue is about Kali Rising, right? She with the necklace of severed heads and the skirt of human arms...and you're starting out with talk about *play*?

Shiva: We are working our way to Kali. I guess the first order of business is to get beyond the idea of play as something trivial or unimportant. We are talking about *serious* play – or maybe I should say, the death of seriousness, so that play is all there is, and therefore it is the modus operandi of your whole life....

Shakti: In other words, I'm always playing?

Shiva: Exactly. But this is not just semantic quibbling. We are not using the word "play" to mean all the other things that people fill their lives with. Instead, they are being asked to drop all the pursuits they are involved in that don't entail a spirit of creative trial and error—that aren't done for the sheer joy of it.

Shakti: That might not leave much.

Shiva: So, that's a testament to how revolutionary and important this shift would be.

Shakti: If I were a human, it might also make me feel overwhelmed. Like there wouldn't be enough of me left for me to recognize myself.... Hmmm....could be.... But this is Tantra. It's not for nothing that it's known as a radical path....In any case, one shouldn't get discouraged.

Shiva: It happens gradually, at the pace you wish. And it's driven by your own spontaneity. The important thing right now is to realize that we are putting play at heart of the spiritual process – that philosophy and spirituality in Tantra are organized around the notion (or maybe the observation) that the universe is a joyous, spontaneous, playful dance. In other words no room there for losing oneself in guilt, punishment, sin, redemption, shame, and all that unending list of what the tantrica would consider time-consuming absurdities.

So, the first principle is that "everything is an experiment." And in keeping with the radical nature of Tantra that means literally *everything*. Life becomes a constant process of discovery, exploration, and, if you collect the data and analyze it as part of your experiment, ever deepening learning.

But all of that will become clearer after we talk about *spontaneity* – and the role of containment.

Principle 2. The dynamic between tapas
(containment) and spanda (the life force) is at the heart
of the process of birth and transformation.

Spanda

Shiva: Tantra is all about enabling spontaneity. We often refer to this with the Sanskrit root word spanda (from which the English *spontaneous* comes [*].) Spanda, the fundamental vibrating quality of everything in the universe, is the tendency to *move* – back and forth if it's the vibrating of a body at rest—or out into action if it's not. We all have that inherent capacity and desire to *act* – to manifest something, our desires, our dreams, our compassion, love, etc.

In fact, that's probably what we all want for ourselves in our deepest "heart of hearts": to be able to live in a totally spontaneous way. After all, isn't that what freedom really means: to express our most genuine impulses, freely and without constraint – in a way that we know is loved, valued, and precisely what is needed from us at that moment?

Shakti: But that's ridiculous. I mean it's not really possible is it? If everyone did that, the world would be chaotic, crazy, and probably downright dangerous, wouldn't it?

Shiva: Notice I said "in a way that you could know that your actions were precisely what was needed from you in that moment." [**] In other words, they have to be vetted.

Shakti: By whom?

Shiva: That's where Kali comes in. Not that She does the vetting, but She is the example of the pure thing – the standard by which vetting is done. She is the most dramatic manifestation of the life force, the upsurge of Nature's essence into manifestation. It's always on point. Actually the word kala (Kali is the feminine form) in Sanskrit means "time." Her timing is impeccable. No hesitation there, or crippling self-consciousness. In fact, she couldn't care less about self. She is the great champion of the needs of the whole. When the time is right, the seed will push up – even through concrete.

If you want to see Her in action, go into a delivery room. Just think about it. For nine months the nurturing aspect of the feminine (not what your Kali in her terrible form represents) builds us a paradise, a sort of personal, ecstasy-inducing flotation tank that we can luxuriate

[*] The vowels of *spanda* are pronounced like those of the first two syllables of *spontaneity*.
[**] It might be helpful for the reader to think of this as the microcosmic manifestation of a macrocosmic force. See also Part II chapter 5, page 171.

in and have all our needs met. Then, suddenly, Kali steps in, and in one fell swoop, rips open the womb, and ejects the newborn into the world. Not much concern for self-interest of either mom or infant it would appear at first glance. But at a deeper level, She is serving the interest of both – perhaps not their self-interest in the narrow sense, but the interest of the growth and evolution of each.

As that Archetype, Kali lives in each person, and She appears at just the right time and says, OK, NOW! That is, if allowed. If She is thwarted, which can be done for awhile, we get out of rhythm with the universe. We then are out of tune. We are holding back. If we continue to do that, She will show up and lop off a few heads (read egos), and push us on through to the next stage.

Figure 1 : Kali in Her terrifying form

Shakti: Like a storm?

Shiva: Or an earthquake. In fact, you might say that right now the earth is in arrears. People have been postponing the needed changes that would ensure that the planet continues to be habitable. So She's beginning to whip up storms, quakes, "disasters" that will rip open the womb and push out into birth the next phase of human development on this planet.

Shakti: I get the birthing part. But the image that is described for Kali is certainly not what most people think of when they think "feminine."

Shiva: Right! Good point. She does not seem feminine in the current westernized human's mythical world. But such goddesses are common in most indigenous cultures – where life was tied up with Nature and her cycles. The modern (or post modern) Eurocentric western psyche has substantially separated itself from Nature. It junked the birthing aspect of the Feminine – it's too unpredictable, and it doesn't "respect" ego accomplishments – is much too willing to smash them when they are in the way of personal development.

Instead people of that type have focused their version of the Feminine on the receptive – the vulnerable, nurturing, Mother Mary. The other side of Mary (i.e., Magdalene) who is strong, outspoken, powerful, has been banished from our inner world – and even from religious iconography.

They really don't want Her around. "She will ruin everything!" (See Pedro Aldodovar film Mala Educacion). Their version of feminism has been selective: women have a choice of donning a business suit and grabbing a briefcase and entering the halls of corporate or government control, or staying at home (or in the classroom, or the nursing station, or the secretarial pool, or fill in the blank) and settling for the role of nurturing and supporting the masculine ego.

Even the prototypical expression of the birthing feminine energy, the actual delivery of a newborn, has increasingly been banished. Obstetricians often find the Kali scene too disruptive. She doesn't go by hospital schedules, She makes a mess – all those smelly fluids and that blood everywhere – and anyway, how can I plan my nine holes of golf when I don't know when I need to be in the delivery room? So better I use my (phallic) scalpel and do this job in a neat, predictable, and efficient way. The result is an absurd percentage of deliveries done by C-Section – far beyond what can be explained by medical necessity. And you think that happens because of some hole, some missing

Shakti: piece, in the concept of the Feminine?

Shiva: Indeed I do. It is an impoverished image of the Feminine. Not that the nurturing aspect of the Feminine is trivial. It is essential. Without nurturance, we all perish. So there's a need to find outside or, more maturely, inside oneself, the other, more yin side of the Feminine, in order to ensure well-being. But simply nurturing, with no evolution, no transformation, is stagnation and we are likely to end up bloated, complacent, and bored.

For transformation is the essence of living systems. Life forms are made up of an interlocking web of biochemical, physiological, electrical, and psychological transformative processes. When this slows significantly, we cease to feel alive. When it stops, we die.

It is only the Kali mode, the birthing aspect of the Feminine that can bring something new into the world. Transformation is not possible without *Her*. In other words, if you cannot access Her, bring her into play, you cannot make any real change. You can "rearrange the deck chairs," so to speak, but you can't come up with a sofa (or a plan to get off the ship before it sinks).

The same principle holds true with the collective psyche. If humanity as a family, a country, or a planet, cannot find, honor, and make room for Her, they merely repeat themselves. Any ostensible change is merely the same old thing in a slightly altered form: old wine in new wineskins. Therefore it should not baffle us that global warming continues unabated as such collective bodies have their meetings, pass resolutions, and by and large fail miserably to alter the general course of events.

Shakti: So when you say we must all, individually and collectively find Her and allow her to act, that includes me?

Shiva: Well, not really. For the most part, you exhibit the Yang Feminine quite nicely. You are it – shakti is the very energy of spanda's expression.

Shakti: But you were talking about Kali...

Shiva: Yes, your alter ego.

Shakti: She's a bit intimidating....

Shiva: That's an understatement.

Shakti: What I mean is that I hesitate to take on the role. Certainly to *look* the part.

Shiva: It seems that humans share that reticence. But refusing to give spanda room to express, not only leads to stagnation and frustration, the She inside will get frustrated and unmanageable and burst forth in ways one might not wish to have to deal with.

Shakti: Like mass murder?

Shiva: That can be a twisted version of it. In your case it is Kali in Her purer form. For most people, i.e., humans, who may have various unaddressed, shadowy stuff cluttering their inner spaces, it can get distorted. But if the personal strikes a little to close to home, they should try looking at the collective: if they don't let Her step forward and birth something truly new for our planetary agenda, humankind faces possible annihilation.

Kali rising is a sort of remedial measure. Her rampage is a response to the squelching of spontaneity. Let's get back to spanda itself: How to live through its action. Then Kali's work is kept to a minimum.

Shakti: I like that better. So how do I know when I'm being genuinely spontaneous and when I'm just telling myself I am? What does it feel like?

Shiva: You do ask good questions. That's one of the big ones. It's easy to pretend to yourself that you are being free, when in fact you are being run by all sorts of habits and fears. But you, personally, don't have to worry about this. With the exception of the tinge of humanness you take on (so that humans can relate to you), you *are* Shakti, the very essence of spanda.

Shakti: I get that. But how do they – humans—tell the difference? Speak to my tinge of humanness.

Shiva: Generous of you. It has to be done through the body. That's why Tantra is often called "embodied spirituality." The "throb" that is the primordial essence of spanda can be felt in your physical being. It's the engine behind your desire to stretch sensually when you first get out the bed on a beautiful day – when you've slept well, eaten well, and aren't fighting fatigue, I should add.

What you responded to when you reached up toward the ceiling was spanda. It comes from deep inside the earthiness of your being.

It is the call to participate joyfully in the coordinated dance of the natural world. Following it gives you a pleasure that is "full bodied," in the fullest sensual sense of the expression. Spanda is that thing, the ignoring of which, makes you feel thwarted in your inner most being. Spanda is what you follow when you have the most delicious sex. Spanda is the spark that ignites the fire of life.

Shakti: Great promo! There should be hoards of humans lining up for that. I'm sold.

Shiva: Well, I'm not surprised. It's what you are: Shakti is the prototypical expression of spanda. And as the essence of that Feminine, you are much more attuned and responsive to it than I am.

Shakti: You mean men don't have it?

Shiva: No, I don't mean that at all. And I assume you are talking about male-bodied humans—which I'm really not, of course. I'm just a god – specifically the archetypal pattern that can throw forth into the mundane human world a manifestation of the most elegant, non-violent yet outrageously sexy masculinity.

Human men, however, have spanda just like female-bodied humans. It's just that their preoccupation (and often nearly exclusive focus on) their Masculine leads them to ignore – or even deny – their Feminine. And spanda is clearly in the feminine department. That's why when a woman says, "I just feel like it is the right thing to do," you're generally better off following her than when a man says the same thing.

Shakti: Let's say I'm a human. When I feel the inner impulse to get up and go to the freezer for a third bowl of chocolate ice cream, is that spanda?

Shiva: Would you really, on checking in with your innermost self, say, "I just feel like this is the right thing to do?"

Shakti: Well, not really.

Shiva: What would you say on that little inner inventory before shuffling off to the fridge?

Shakti: Well I'm leaning a bit heavily on my "tinge of humanness" here, but I'd say it's a bad habit that would probably (if I were in a human body) leave me feeling yucky and bloated the next morning.

Shiva: Sounds like you don't really have a problem identifying spanda.

Shakti: Well, I shouldn't, right? But, if I were a human I suspect that I wouldn't find it so easy, or, I wouldn't want to admit it, if I did. It would sort of spoil the fun.

Shiva: Does it really? Feeling yucky and bloated doesn't sound like such a fun fest. I'd say that following spanda is a much more fool-proof path to more fun.

Shakti: Following what really feels right inside – what emerges from your essence –doesn't always lead to delightful experiences, either. It can also get you in uncomfortable jams.

Shiva: Uncomfortable perhaps, but I'll bet not boring – and I'll wager you feel more alive than when you don't follow that little spark.

Shakti: True – and the Kali part of me is in total agreement!

Shiva: The tantric path will go for "more alive" every time.

Shakti: OK. I can see that. And I'm on board. But what is the humble human supposed to do with the habit that gets her out of the chair and off to the fridge. Unless you can help her with that, it's pretty much all theory, as far as I can see.

Shiva: So glad you asked! That leads us into the exploration of our next foundational principle: the use of *tapas*. [*]

Tapas

Shiva: You feel that impulse to get up and go to the fridge for your ice cream fix. (Your average human seems to adore ice cream!) You have already established that it is not spanda. And you have already made a commitment to applying the technique of tapas here. So, *as soon as you feel the impulse*, you relax. You breathe. You look the impulse (rooted in habit) in the face, and say quietly and calmly, "no thanks." You don't "try hard", you don't berate yourself for your weakness, you simply bow out. "Thanks, I think I'll sit this one out."

[*] See appendix E

A habit is like a weed. It's tough and doesn't give up without a fight. It wants to perpetuate itself, and it does so by gaining energy – a charge within you – every time you carry out the action it dictates. By the same token, every time you demur, every time you simply breathe and relax and decline to perform the expected action, it weakens.

There is a Gandhian quality to this technique. It's passive resistance. You don't fight back. You simply relax and breathe. Now the habit morphs from a weed into a wild animal. It wants its energetic charge. It will have its ice cream. It doesn't like the containment that tapas creates. It begins to thrash about and rattle its cage.

You are the stage upon which this drama is being enacted. You feel the internal turmoil of the enraged, thwarted habit. But you don't let that disturb you, because you knew, more or less, what to expect. Like an expert horse trainer "breaking" a colt, you bide your ti me, stay calm, understand, and wait.

Eventually something dramatically shifts. The energy that would have been expended in carrying out the habitual action, unable to flow through its customary course, breaks out of that groove, and blazes a new trail through your energetic body. Now the energy can be used for something entirely new. It is a spanda moment!

You come alive in a new way. Often some higher energy center (chakra) gets a jolt of energy from the rising charge. Perhaps it's your heart center and you feel an opening of compassion, understanding for what your fellow humans struggle with. Or your Throat Chakra, and you feel the creative juices flowing and pick up your guitar, or paint brush, or hammer and saw, or whatever. The released energy powers an increment of transformation, and you are, in some small way at least, a new and more radiant being.

Tapas, it is said, is what gives me my glow (which is dramatic in my better moments!) There is no translation of the term into English – at least none that works. Some use the word "discipline" in an attempt to render tapas in the English language. But that's all wrong. The idea of discipline among the English speaking peoples is usually "doing what you don't want to do." In other words , forcing yourself to go against your inclinations. It's the white-knuckle thing. Grit you teeth and tighten up your body, and push through it. But clearly, that is not at all how tapas works.

Tapas is a simple but brilliant technique for *enabling* spanda. By containing the energy that would otherwise be expended by rote habits, that energy can " rise" to originate new, unexpected actions—in other words, to "birth" something heretofore not seen or imagined. That is the quality of the spontaneous life. Oddly enough, that spontaneity is not possible without the containment provided by tapas.

Musicians know this. Charlie Parker was asked how his jazz renditions could be so free and unfettered. He said, you practice, and do scales, and exercises for years, and "then, one day you just rear back and *wail!*" His music soared, and he came to be called, Bird.

Classical Indian music understands this principle, and unlike its Western counterpart provides a structure, or container via the structure of the raga – but within which improvisation can flourish. Every parent knows that a small child will play best – most creatively and spontaneously – in a play pen.

Shakti: I thought that tapas was a little food thing you get at Spanish bars.

Shiva: I feel like you're trying to trivialize what I'm saying. But no matter; I'll respond. In fact, the word *tapa* in Spanish also means lid, or what you put on the pot to contain the food – and its connotation is that there are small amounts. In other words, it's about declining to eat a huge amount just because it tastes good, and instead, trying other delicacies. So it's consistent with its linguistic cousin in Sanskrit, which is clearly related to Indo European languages such as Spanish.

Shakti: OK. I confess to being a bit resistant to practicing what you are preaching here. I guess that I'm more open to spanda while you resonate more with tapas. I'm just having a bit of a problem buying into the sweeping implications. So you are saying that you can just "apply tapas" to all your unwanted habits, and presto! You are a different person? Sounds too good to be true. And you know what they say: "When it sounds too good to be true, usually it is too good to be true." Well, that's not really what I said. At least that's not what I meant. You don't just do wholesale tapas and change everything. If you changed all your habits, your whole personality would change, since that's all personality is anyway, just a "bundle of habits." Human beings for sure would have a lot of trouble with that, since they are pretty attached to their personalities – especially those who are most westernized, self-important, ego-oriented. Maybe that would knock them for such a loop they would never get a solid enough footing again to continue down their path......

Anyhow, that's not how tapas works. If you want it to be effective, you choose one habit. And not just at random. You have to choose one that is "ripe." It's like a piece of fruit. When you pluck it, it is full of juice – the juice is the energy you get that used to fuel the habit, but is now yours to do delightful things with. But that won't work if the habit is not at a point where you are ready to give it up – ripe.

If you are not ready to give up your nightly pint of ice cream, forget it. Don't try to use tapas, because it would be premature.

Shakti: How do you know when it's "ripe," as you call it?

Shiva: A little bit of self-scrutiny is needed here. There comes a time when something changes with your attitude toward a habitual action. For months, maybe, or years, you have been doing something and really enjoying it. Then on a subtle level – where you'd rather not look – there's a shift in how it feels. It still tastes the same, for example, but it's just not as pleasurable. I want my ice cream, I insist on my ice cream, no one is going to take my ice cream away from me, but the secret truth that I don't want to admit is that I am really tired of that chocolate ice cream every night. In fact, if I really admitted the truth, I am a bit sick of it. Now the habit is ripe.

Shakti: So what if my ice cream habit is not ripe, what do I do?

Shiva: Keep eating it. The time to work with it will come. But one request: As long as you are eating it, please enjoy it! After all, life on earth is just a parade of habits that people need to ripen up, and if you don't enjoy the process, you are missing out on the joy of life. It's a fine art: to allow consciousness without obstructing joy.

Shakti: You seem to have this tapas thing down to a science.

Shiva: Indeed. That is actually my forte. I am known for my lingam [*], but the truth is, this tapas, the testicular aspect of my being is equally, or perhaps even more, important.

Shakti: Uh....did I miss something? Your what? *Testicular?* As in *testicle?*

Shiva: Exactly. That's where we go next......I mean that's the next subject.

[*]   The lingam is a symbol of the descending ray of light as well as of the phallus. See glossary.

FOUNDATIONAL MEDITATION I

Breathing Up and Down the Spine

Establish a comfortable upright position. If sitting on the floor doesn't work for you, then sit in a chair, preferably forward, toward the edge, so that you can maintain a normally erect spine (with gentle curves forward at the lower back and neck).

Once you have found a posture that is comfortable and stable enough to sustain for ten minutes or so, settle into it, and allow all the muscles that are not necessary to maintain the position to relax. You might wish to start at the top of the head with the muscles of the scalp, then the forehead, then the muscles around the eyes, next the cheeks, etc. allowing each to release its tension. Continue down the body: jaw, neck, shoulders, arms, torso, pelvis, hips, legs, and feet.

Entering other realms of consciousness is best done gradually, moving from gross to subtler to subtlest. Once you feel your body is as relaxed as it can be today, turn your attention to the breath. First, simply observe the breath. As much as possible, avoid altering your breath at this stage. Rather merely notice what you can about how your habitual breath functions. Is it deep or shallow? Does it expand all the way down into your lower abdomen? To your pelvis? Or does it limit itself to the chest? Or only to the upper chest? Just take note.

Next notice whether it is irregular or smooth and rhythmic. See if you can identify a pattern. Now, examine the juncture between inhalation and exhalation. Is there a smooth and continuous transition, or does the breath stop here for a time. After that, look at the juncture between exhalation and inhalation.

Once you have studied your breath for a minute or two, you may then begin to gently encourage the breath to move up and down the spine. This is done by moving the attention slowly and steadily along the course of the spinal column. Where you bring your attention, the subtle energy tends to follow. Though we speak of the breath here, we are actually attending to the flow of subtle energy or *prana*. The breath is the most straightforward way to guide or shift subtle energy. The yogis say, "If *prana* is the kite, the breath is the string."

Yet the breath should not be forced, only *allowed* to follow the attention. (He does not try to force Her, He merely attracts Her toward Him with His light of

Consciousness). So starting at the tip of the lower spine, sweep up the length of the spine slowly, as inhalation occurs. Imagine that the sweep of your attention is like a spotlight moving upwards. Time the speed of the movement to reach the top of the head as you complete the inhalation.

Now spend three to five minutes following up and down the spine, coordinating the sweep of your attention with the flow of the breath. Inhaling up, exhaling down. As you inhale, with your mind's eye move up the spine, as though you are examining it in minutest detail, moving up with inhalation to the crown of the head, and then reversing: down with exhalation to the lowest tip of the spine.

As your exhalation ends, you reach the lowest point along the spine, then, without interruption, begin the upward course. Encourage the breath to be regular, without jerks or pauses. Allow inhalation to flow into exhalation and exhalation to flow into inhalation, so there is no pause or interruption. The maximal expansion in the chest should be at the lower edge of the rib cage. (Diaphragmatic breathing [*])

Notice the shifts that occur in your awareness, your sense of self, and your level of vitality as you continue this breath.

There are other versions of this practice. For example the Taoist version continues over the head after inhalation is complete to exhale down the front of the body. The more typically tantric version is what is offered here.

[*] See Science of Breath

PRINCIPLES 3 & 4

Shiva for his Divine Consort, Shakti

Principle 3. *The human being is of a dual nature,
Masculine and Feminine, and each of those likewise are of
two aspects: two aspects of the Feminine, and, similarly,
two of the Masculine. Thus are there four.*

Shakti: You were about to tell me about your testicles, or something like that.

Shiva: The testicular...

Shakti: But before that, could you just clear up this business of "Masculine" and "Feminine". Usually, if I have my English straight, they are just adjectives: something is masculine, or feminine. You seem to be using them as nouns. What is "a Masculine?"

Shiva: I know, you are right. It's awkward. But we are stuck in this century – and since we have "gone global"—with trying to talk about these matters in this highly unsuitable language....

Shakti: You mean English?

Shiva: Yes.

Shakti: I do miss the gracefulness of Sanskrit, or even Pali – it was OK...

Shiva: Or even Malayalam. I mean, there's no decent word in English for *prana*, or tapas, as I said before, or even *shakti*.

Shakti: You're telling me? I feel like I'm suddenly a non-entity. ....

Shiva: I know, but we have to work with what we've got. And it would be silly to pretend that we're having these conversations solely for our own good. Clearly they are meant to resonate with the masses, and when you want to reach global masses, English is the trick these days. So, I hope you will understand—I have to take certain liberties with the language.

Shakti: I totally understand, but I still need an explanation of what it means.

Shiva: "The Masculine" means the *masculine principle*, in the world, or the cosmos—in a word, (though not one everybody in our broadened audience will understand) *me*. And the feminine principle is, of course, *you*.

Shakti: Oh. That brings it down to the familiar.

Shiva: You might say.

Shakti: So we each have "a Masculine" and "a Feminine."

Shiva: Not *we*, dear, *they*. As god and goddess we are the *pure* Masculine (I) and Feminine (You). That's our definition, *raison d'etre*. Humans, bless them, are *both*. That is to say, each one of them is both Masculine and Feminine. But they identify so much with the one of us that matches their anatomical equipment, that they forget their other side.

Shakti: By "other side" you mean....

Shiva: Actually, *literally* their other side. Their right side is *me*, their left *you*. Curious how they manage to ignore this. Even those who have studied yoga seem to forget that the right breath – associated with the right main energy channel, pingala, is what activates the left brain – which they generally do seem to associate with their linear, rational, more masculine side. And of course, You likewise on the left, with the left channel and the right brain.

Which, of course is why I am sometimes depicted (see illustration on page 43) as the ardhanarishwara, the half-and-half god—masculine on the right and feminine on the left. By the way, my apologies to you – I'm not sure why it's "Shiva depicted as half and half" rather than "Shakti depicted as half and half....."

Shakti: Good question. Why is it?

Shiva: Uh.....I really don't know. Maybe just a quirk of history. Someone did it once, and others followed suit for no good reason.....

Shakti: Baloney. You know better than that. It's pure male chauvinism, and you know it.

Shiva: OK, OK. You are probably right....

Shakti: Probably?!...I...(stops, and shifts her tone). How would you feel about "The half and half deity?"

Shiva: Sure... (then, hesitantly) Uh...we were talking about how little awareness there is of the dual, masculine/feminine nature among humans....

Shakti: Yes, why doesn't it register in their awareness? It's really a bummer. Few of the men own me; that's for sure....

Shiva: That's true, and related, no doubt to the question of how they title the pictures of the Ardhanarishvara. There's no small amount of mi-

Figure 2: Ardhanarishvara, The Half & Half Diety

sogyny and, I suspect, a generous portion of homophobia in men – especially the European/Euroamerican variety. They seem pretty set against acknowledging their feminine. Too bad, since they are not owning their *power* in the process, but they don't get that.

Beyond that, I think that it's also a resistance to allowing us – you and me – to freely merge within them. As we've said, that would catapult them into quite a different reality. And virtually all humans are afraid of change....

Shakti: That makes sense. Seems like they're struggling. Is there any way we can help them?

Shiva: Yes, dear: by sloughing off a lot of the garbage they've foisted off on us and emerging as our pure and pristine selves...

Shakti: How do we do that?

Shiva: That's what this dialogue is for. Of course it needs to be duplicated within each of them. We are sort of at their mercy. For us to re-emerge as marriageable partners, we need their individual and collective participation. Gods and goddesses can't morph themselves unaided – unfortunately. Or maybe fortunately. We wouldn't want some sort of theocratic totalitarianism – after all, the earthly realm is there for the evolution of consciousness...

Shakti: Careful. It's also there for the flowering of Gaia.

Shiva: Granted. But there is a role for the human and her/his search for fuller consciousness...

Shakti: I think that happens when he/she realizes that he/she has a place in the ecosystems of Earth, and learns to fill that niche responsibly and humbly.

Shiva: Touche.

Shakti: But back to your testicles – which are attractive after all....

Shiva: (blushes and seems flustered) Ah, yes.....well, we're getting there. I mean as keeper of the tapas, the structure and container of this discussion.....

Shakti: Sorry to interrupt again but I thought that our observer—and our readers – our "third eye" who is always watching – no privacy here – was to do that....

Shiva: No, not at all. I am the containment expert. That's the testicular function – that's what they do, of course – contain, protect. Biologically, for those fully immersed in the material world, they protect the genetic material....

Shakti: Half of it.

Shiva: Right. Half of it....anyway, you get the idea.

Shakti: I'm not sure I do. What is the idea?

Shiva: You are flustering me! I was trying to maintain the thread of the discussion. Before I talk about my dual role as testicular and phallic, I wanted to make sure to emphasize that human nature includes both masculine and feminine parts. Otherwise, it gets confusing, because I'm about to explain that each of those parts – the Masculine and the Feminine – also has two parts....

Shakti: The two aspects of the Masculine being the phallic and the testicular.

Shiva: Right

Shakti: OK. So the testicular is that which has to do with containment and tapas – which is itself a kind of containment.

Shiva: Exactly.

Shakti: You haven't said anything about the phallic.

Shiva: No but it's not hard to guess.

Shakti: OK. Let me try: the phallic is about penetration.

Shiva: Clearly. But not just in the physical sense. Not even primarily in the physical sense. I mean these anatomically oriented labels are just used because the physical function so eloquently portrays the subtler psychological and even spiritual nature of the masculine and the feminine.

Shakti: As though the material, embodied version is a sculptural representation of the multi leveled spectrum of manifestations that span all the realities of the universe.

Shiva: That's very good!

Shakti: I'm supposed to be learning aren't I?

Shiva: Yes, but not so much or so fast that you upstage me! Despite its image of force and strength, the confidence of the masculine can be a bit fragile, you know....

Shakti: Sorry. I forgot. I'll keep that in mind.

Shiva: So. Where was I?

Shakti: Still in your scrotum.

Shiva: Really. This is a philosophical discussion.

Shakti: I do love embodiment.

Shiva: Well, I do too, but can't we approach it from the philosophical?

Shakti: I realize that is *your* way. But it's not mine. I don't feel at all that the embodied is in any way inferior, "mundane," or even less dignified, for that matter. And I definitely feel that it's more beautiful. Hence my continual willingness to go back to your testicles.

Shiva: (Takes a deep breath). OK. Seems we've pretty much covered – or uncovered, judging by the way I feel at the moment – my reproductive organs and how they reflect the prototypical qualities of the masculine. Though maybe I should add a little disclaimer: the proper use of the phallic is not violent.

Shakti: How do you define violence?

Shiva: Well, in this context, I'd say violation is entry without invitation – or at least permission..

Shakti: That sounds respectful and in a way I like it. But since you've said that, and since I believe that you *mean* it, it is safe for me to say now that sometimes the feminine likes to be seduced into offering that permission – or even to be "taken," as long as her masculine counterpart is damn sure that she wants him.

Shiva: (Sounds worried and nervous) This gets *very* complicated.

Shakti: Did I ever pretend that I – that the Feminine—was not complicated?

Shiva: Probably – often. If it made you look inviting….

Shakti: (laughs) OK. You got me there. But, in any case, I accept your disclaimer – for the moment.

Shiva: Thank you. Can we turn now to the bipartite nature of the Feminine….

Shakti: Good timing. I am curious as to what anatomical structures you are going to associate with the two aspects of me….In fact, I'm curious about what you are going to say are the two aspects of the Feminine.

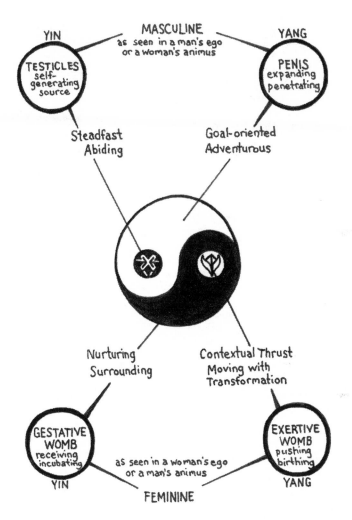

Figure 3: Four Gender "Modes"
(Adapted from Haddon, Genia Pauli, *Uniting Sex, Self, and Spirit*)

Shiva: Well, actually, I should think that you could guess – since aside from your commonly sweet and receptive – and very nurturing – nature, there are moments (as we have just seen), when you can step forward with an, uh….how should I tactfully say this…*assertiveness* that is most breathtaking.

Shakti: Sounds like you're back to the Kali thing.

Shiva: Right, though Kali is an extreme version of it. Let's just say the "birthing energy".

Shakti: Oh! So you mean the *womb*! But wouldn't that be what nurtures?

Shiva: It is. The prototypical example of nurturing – for nine months. But then, when the time is right, nurturing gives way to that consummate active feminine performance: birthing. So for the Feminine, it's the same organ that embodies both feminine "gears," the passive nurturing and receptive, or, let's say, *yin*, and the active birthing and assertive, *yang*.

Shakti: Yin? Yang? That's neither English nor Sanskrit. Seems a little random to me.

Shiva: I know. But again there's nothing in English proper that carries the shade of meaning we need here. Besides, the terms yin and yang have pretty much already made their way into English – and we have staked out our intended territory as global.

Shakti: OK. I can go with yin and yang – Chinese philosophy always seemed like a well-embodied approach to me – practical and down to earth.

Shiva: The terms have been used to distinguish the two aspects of the Masculine and the two aspects of the Feminine (see Fig. 3, Gender Modes). It works: otherwise it gets impossibly confusing – the dual nature of a dual nature.

Shakti: Thank you. It was getting a little too abstract for me. But it seems odd that I get only one organ, while you get two. It feels a little like another diminishment or trivialization of the Feminine….

Shiva: Not at all. It just reflects Your flexibility…. and uh…. (takes a big breath)… changeability….And that's not a put-down. You have to admit that it's one of your major attributes, the capacity to change at the drop of a hat....

Shakti: Umm. (with an edge in her voice) Yes....

Shiva: That allows the Feminine to counter the "consistency hobgoblin of small minds" as an English speaker once wrote.

Shakti: (appeased) That is true.

Shiva: The uterus as the epitome of the Feminine is also perfect because it is *hidden*, out of view, so to speak. In stark contrast to my own primary anatomical male attributes.

Shakti: I will agree that the difference there is dramatic enough to be significant.

Shiva: And I know that you like your privacy....

Shakti: And why not?

Shiva: No reason at all....But it has led to some....shall we say interesting confrontations.

Shakti: What are you talking about?

Shiva: I am recalling what happened in the forest several thousand years ago when we were living there, you in your Parvati guise and me as your faithful spouse.....

Shakti: Oh.

Shiva: May I retell that for those who may not be aware of it?

Shakti: If you must....

Shiva: It does demonstrate the contrast between your two – both remarkable and indispensable – modes of function....

Shakti: OK. Go ahead.

Shiva: Here is the story, in the precise words with which it has long been told in South Asia:

Shiva and Parvati lived in a lovely hermitage in the forest. Life was a joy there. One day while Shiva was away, Parvati decided to take a bath. She told their servant: "If anyone comes, don't let them in, I am going to take my bath."

Not long after, Shiva returned. The servant at the door said, "Excuse me, but you can't go in right now."

"What?" Shiva asked, surprised.

"You can't enter, Parvati is bathing."

"What?!" Shiva responded with disbelief and annoyance. "What do you mean, I can't enter. This is my house...."

"But, Parvati...."

"...and she is my wife!"

With that, Shiva flung the door open and strode inside. Parvati, startled, pulled her towel around herself, and rebuked him. "What are you doing? I asked not to be disturbed!"

"Don't be silly, woman." He replied. "You are my wife!"

Parvati was angered. The next day, she did tapas and appealed to Surya, god of the sun. "Please," she pleaded, "Send me a son that will protect me and safeguard my privacy."

In no time at all, he was there. Though small, he was already on his feet, armed, strong of heart and ready to defend his mother. "Don't worry, Mother," he said. "I will take care of it."

Parvati immediately stationed her new protector at the door and went about having her bath. As fate would have it, no sooner had she done so than Shiva returned home and found the pint-sized warrior standing firmly at the gate.

"Who are you?" Asked Shiva, a bit amused and a bit irritated.

"Who are *you*?" Asked the boy.

"I am Shiva," said the god, now thoroughly outraged, and in no mood to humor the impudent youth.

"Well, whoever you are, it doesn't matter. You can't come in. My mother is taking a bath."

"Your *mother*? And just who is your mother?" Shiva snapped at the boy.

"Parvati," he answered. "Stand back!" he added.

Losing his patience, Shiva stepped forward and grabbed at the boy, aiming to send him on his way. But in a flash, he was yelping in pain, for his young adversary had landed a few swift blows.

He retreated in astonishment. Reappraising the boy, he decided this called for firmer action and a united front.

Soon Shiva was returning with reinforcements: Nandi, his faithful retainer, and another helper were close behind. Together, they closed in on their foe, intending to seize and disarm him. But within moments they were, all three, backing off, and nursing their bruises. The little fellow was fierce and *fast*.

The three men withdrew a short distance to regroup. Shiva was not only angry, but embarrassed and humiliated. "This is ridiculous!" he exclaimed. "We cannot let this nasty little interloper take over the house! We have to do something."

After considering the alternatives, Shiva decided extreme measures were called for: "Although it is not, strictly speaking, fair, I must conclude that we have no recourse. You attack him from the front, and while his attention is so diverted, I will slip up behind and finish him off."

And that was what they did. Soon the little creature was stretched out on the ground, his head lopped off and lying beside him.

Almost at that precise moment, the door swung open, and Parvati stepped out to find her son lying decapitated before her.

"What have you *done*?!" She screamed, her eyes flashing fire as she scanned the men standing before her and found Shiva standing over the boy with a bloody sword in his hand. "You have killed my child!" she cried out in horror and grief. And she fell to the ground beside the little one, putting her arms around him and weeping over his corpse.

She keened with grief, and then she screamed with fury. And with each volley of cries, the volume mounted. The men felt as if the very heavens would fall on them, as her wailing shook the earth. In fact, the skies darkened, and countless shaktis fell down from above like fragments of furious lightning bolts.

Though at first the men stood frozen to the spot as they witnessed the chaos that their actions had unleashed, they soon turned and ran. The further they went the more obvious it became that the pandemonium was not localized. The whole world was shaking and threatening to disintegrate.

As they huddled to protect themselves and try to think what they should do, Shiva said, "I must go to Indra, king of the gods. Surely he can help."

But when Shiva approached Indra, Indra merely shook his head. "What can I do?" he asked. "You should not have angered her so."

"So what do I do now?" Shiva asked desperately. "The very survival of the world is at stake!"

"You are right." replied Indra. "So you must find some way to appease her."

Shiva and his cohorts hurried back to the hermitage, traversing scenes of devastation and suffering visible on all sides.

When they found the still grieving Parvati, Shiva threw himself at her feet. "Please, he said, I repent my actions. Please forgive me. What can I do to set this right?"

"I only want my child back," Parvati wept.

Shiva and his henchmen huddled again in the mounting din of storms, quakes and destruction. "I have an idea," Shiva said. "I am not sure that it will work. But we have to try something. The first live animal we see, let us cut off its head and bring it back here."

The first was an elephant. The head was quickly removed and hastily brought back to the scene of the crime. Using his *siddhis*, Shiva united it to the boy's body, and lo and behold, he sat up and breathed! Parvati was overjoyed. She embraced her son and, despite his odd appearance, like any mother she found him adorable. The sounds of fury abated, the sun returned to the sky, and peace prevailed.

To this very day, you will find on every kitchen hearth in India a little statue of Ganesh, to remind all that peace in the home is maintained by respecting and tending to *Her* feelings and needs.

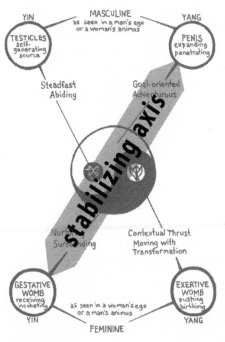

Figure 4: the Stabilzing Axis in the Gender Mode Realm

Shakti: It sort of makes me seem like a monster, doesn't it?

Shiva: Quite the contrary. It's that wildness-with-a-purpose lurking behind serene sweetness and beauty that makes you so mysterious and fascinating.

Shakti: I love it when you flatter me.

Shiva: (knowingly) I know.

Shakti: And I hate your smugness.

Shiva: I know that, too – At least since the events of the story we just heard.

Shakti: Well, all's well that ends well.

Shiva: And it did end well.....with, I might concede, some major humbling
– and transformation on my part.

Shakti: Was there anything else that you wanted to say about our dual natures?

Shiva: Just that there are two ways in which we relate or engage: one is what
we might call stereotypical Masculine relating to stereotypical Feminine. What is the social norm in most cultures.

Shakti: You mean the big, strong, macho guy and the sweet, yielding spouse?

Shiva: Yes.

Shakti: That's what I suspected.

Shiva: You don't find that appealing.

Shakti: An understatement.

Shiva: But it has its value.

Shakti: And that is?

Shiva: Well, the nurturing Feminine is what is responsible for the sustenance
of the world. That, the Yin Feminine, is also receptivity – without
which no human could take nurturance in, or learn, or inhale—or be
enlivened by the Divine.

Shakti: True. I am no doubt of utmost importance. (She smiles and spoofs a pose – as though for the paparazzi). But what about Him – the Yang Masculine, the phallic aspect of your makeup –the part of you that led you to bushwhack Ganesh, getting you into such trouble in our little story a few minutes ago?

Shiva: The part whose value you were questioning?

Shakti: The same.

Shiva: He....I – or at least that half of me – is what provides adventurousness, curiosity, goal-directed effort. Without that we wouldn't make fortunes, conquer new frontiers....

Shakti: I think you are incriminating yourself...

Shiva: What do you mean?

Shakti: Haven't you heard? The world is already over conquered, and the fortune thing has sort of imploded on itself – started to look greedy, self-defeating, actually rather silly and adolescent....

Shiva: OK, I understand what you are saying. But there are other versions of it that shouldn't be discounted.

Shakti: Such as?

Shiva: Well, the capacity to *penetrate* is what makes it possible to enter into a different space. For example, my reknown capacity for seeing into – *into* the essence of a matter. Or to enter you, not just sexually, but to enter into your reality, your inner world.

Shakti: And you think you do that?

Shiva: Only partially and sporadically. But when I do, I can offer clarification for you, sometimes making the difference between your wasting your awesome creative power and using it to great benefit....

Shakti: I will give you credit for that – even gratitude.

Shiva: Thanks. Notice that it's no longer merely containment that we are talking about here, but insight and discrimination – discerning or distinguishing between one option and another.

Shakti: So you are saying the containment is the "testicular" and the penetrating insight is the phallic.

Shiva: Right.

Shakti: I rejoice in both – in their anatomical, physical form and function as well as the wider application of them. I, being the personification of the Feminine, receive this support from your pure Masculine, and hope that our archetypal existence hovering over the masses of humanity can inspire humans to similar collaboration between Masculine and Feminine – inside themselves as well as out.

But I do feel compassion for women – female-bodied humans – who should be able to drop comfortably back into their Feminine and rely on men to support them and the use of their Yang Feminine— their power. But *can't*. It's a sorry state of affairs.

Fortunately, they have courageously forged ahead by discovering and bringing into play their own masculine capacities – testicular and phallic. That's great! But it's a little sad, too. It sort of sets back the union project on the social front: the true marriage of the Feminine in a woman and the Masculine in a man.

Shiva: Indeed. But that was never the main point. The ultimate purpose of this human comedy/dance between the genders, was, if you will allow me my license as a god, to further the *inner* marriage. That's where the real foundation for transformation on the planet must be built. Searching to "perfect" the outer marriage, while having an inner divorce – or inner "domestic violence," is at best futile.

Shakti: I'd say let's underscore and celebrate that! It's one point on which we are in total agreement! I may bicker with you sometimes to remind you of my feelings and needs and my power but, hey! You're a prince! Those human men who are exploiting women – trying to enslave them to steal their power, preying on their natural desire and need to nurture….(her voice is rising).

We better change the subject, I can feel myself beginning to morph into my Kali mode….

Shiva: As the keeper of tapas here, I might feel compelled to agree with that hesitation on your part, except for the fact that I am beginning to suspect that this is a job for Her – for Kali, I mean. All the signals have been given, the supports put in place, and still there is a very dominant, relatively blind element on planet Earth that continues to pursue its stubborn course. I – we – rely on the Yang Feminine's unerring sense of timing and Her knowledge that "that's enough!" and on Her – You—to blow the whistle. So if She feels that its whistle blowing time, I say, let Her have at it!

Shakti: When the time has come, I can relish the lopping off of heads – at least that part of me can—but at the moment, I find myself wishing that humans could just get it together before that is necessary....

Shiva: Probably the greatest obstacle to that is men not owning their own Yang Feminine.

Shakti: Why do you say that?

Shiva: Well, the Yang Feminine is power. As far as our tantric understanding goes, it is the only power.

Shakti: What about military might – is that Yang Feminine?

Shiva: Generally, no, at least how it is done in present times. But it's not power either.

Shakti: Why not?

Shiva: The origin of the English word *power* is the Old French for "to be able." That would make it the ability to manifest something—actually close to its signification in Tantra: to create. During its sojourn in England, however, the word power assumed new colorations: "possession of control, authority, or influence over others." The way it is most commonly used now in English. This brings it toward the kind of brute force that you are talking about, which is ordinarily used, not to create, but rather to squelch or take over someone else's creativity.

Shakti: Why don't they use their own?

Shiva: Ah! That's the crucial point: Because it's feminine! And men, having bought their own misogynistic propaganda so thoroughly over the centuries—and told themselves so long that to be like a woman is to "debase" themselves—would literally rather die than do so! This conditioning is so engrained and their inner voices scream at them with such fury when they reach into their Feminine, that they shrink back and desist. (The thing a man hates most is to be ridiculed.) So they have no access to their own power. They refuse to, because it is part of Her, and they *will not go there.*

The irony is they have become weak because they are afraid of being like a woman, who, they made themselves believe, is weak! Thus they have brainwashed themselves to the point that they are powerless.

And the irony deepens even further: They have demeaned women and exploited them so that they can be in control. Now they are "in power" – at least nominally. But they can't really live up to their role because in actuality they *have* no power. It's a sham. At this point, despite their desperate efforts to avoid ridicule, they are at great risk of becoming a laughingstock because they are "those in power who have no power!" They are fakes.

Therefore they must exert Herculean effort to keep this truth from coming to light. And it's not easy. First they must make sure that the Yang Feminine voice is not allowed anywhere near. Like Bush's "free speech zones," she must be permitted to express herself only in safe locations. The strong black woman,[*] for example, can be a nanny (where she is often the power that holds a household together), or maybe a civil servant, if it's a lower echelon job. But never, *never* is the voice of Kali to be allowed in the Corporate Board Room. A woman can enter, but only if she dons a suit, carries a brief case, and plays the role of an ersatz man. A true Yang Feminine presence? Why, She would stand, look the men up and down, and ask, "You are spraying our neighborhoods with WHAT? Are you OUT OF YOUR MINDS?" She would become the ultimate whistle blower, and would walk out of that boardroom with a string of severed heads hanging around her neck.

So, no Yang Feminine energy. Much as a dictator who fears his opposition, that presence must be purged from the land. No image of a Yang Feminine goddess is to be seen, and if it is, it is mandatory that it carry a caption that indicates that this object of worship is that of a primitive, nearly subhuman, people.

The eradication must extend into the last and most ancient of Her strongholds: the delivery room, where Kali's power is normally felt in its most raw and unadulterated form.

---

[*] At the risk of being called a racist, I consider the woman of color to most frequently and most clearly serve as the holder of the Yang Feminine in recent times. I suspect this is at least in part because she has so frequently been kept out of the "halls of power (sic)" that her expression of the Yang Feminine is not felt as a threat to the established order.

Shakti: You get really worked up when you launch into this, don't you?

Shiva: Yeah, maybe I was chanelling a little of your Yang Feminine energy there. But most of my attentiveness to the issue is my tapas/testicular responses coming to the fore. This violence—and its cause—is one of the main threats to you.

Shakti: Well, thank you, my dear. It's a comfort to know that you are on it.

But is this total disconnect from their Feminine sustainable for men? How can they keep going?

Shiva: Not very well, and not very long. They often die young – doing themselves in by trying to live without nurturance or power. They would probably go sooner were it not for the kindnesses of women who are willing to put up with their fakery and give them the nurturance and the power they won't access inside themselves..

One of the most telling breakdowns is in the arena of sexuality. A little appreciated fact is that the penis will not become erect without the participation of spanda. Yet spanda is part of man's feminine nature – actually part of his *Yang* Feminine nature. So, as with the rest of his power, this sinks out of reach if he is disconnected from Her. So he becomes not only powerless, but also sexually impotent—the ultimate humiliation for him.

It's not an easy place to be in. We must feel compassion for the individual man who finds himself in this dilemma. He did not personally engineer all the cultural shifts and social changes that led to this. But he suffers the effects. And he isn't happy.

In fact, he often responds to the impossible situation by becoming angry – and not only angry but rageful. He finds himself – often inexplicably for him – in a chronic impotent rage.

Shakti: I'm getting the point about stymied movement, stuckness, overdue change, time for Kali to step in….

Shiva: Well, when you feel the need to swing into Kali gear, and I, as the tender of tapas, give you the all-clear signal, what inevitably emerges is a juicy, very high energy shift—a *transformative* moment. That, if you look at the diagrammatic summary of all this gender mode stuff, is the diagonal axis running from upper right to lower left.

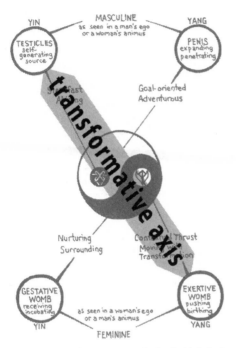

Figure 5: The Transformative Axis in the Gender Mode Realm

At some point, a bit earlier in this conversation, I began to explain that there are two major ways that the Masculine and Feminine interact: the stereo-typical Yang Masculine with Yin Feminine was the first [*]. But this—this *transformative* possibility—the Yin Masculine (testicular/tapas) with the Yang Feminine (birthing/uterine exertive) is the other. This second axis is what is warming up right now. It's already being worked, and it looks like its going to be worked a lot in the coming few years. After we do enough transforming for Her – you – to feel that we've "caught up" and are back on track, we will pre-sumably settle in to another replenishing, goal pursuing age of peace, tranquil-ity and delight – in other words, back to predominantly the stabilizing axis.

[*] This interaction, which sustains, is identified with Vishnu as the Masculine and Lakshmi as the Feminine and is identified with the stabilizing or sustaining axis, whereas the relationship between Shiva as masculine and Shakti as feminine is what characterizes the transformative axis. Those whose focus is on abundance, good health, and success in life will be devotees of Vishnu and Lak-shmi (Vaishnavism), while those whose interest is in transformation will be dedicated to Shiva and Shakti as the personification of that.

Shakti: From what you say, I suspect we'll be ready for a bit of that for a while. And I am ready for a bit right now. My head is spinning with all this talk of abstractions. Can't you remind me of *my* Yin Feminine?

Shiva: You're right. I got carried away. Hmm....let's see.....Try this:
When I sink into Your eyes, I fall
deeper and deeper until I alight at last
in the land of milk and honey,
in that valley below, where
the darkest, most forested spot is the sweetest.
There at the entrance is a single flower,
within which is hidden the twin mysteries
of ecstasy and power. I, like a honeybee
am drawn inexorably into its folds...

Shakti: That works for me..... Don't you think we should take a little "time together" break?

Shiva: It's clearly our duty.

Principle 4. *Tantra operates in various realities,
the "normal world" being the least real.*

Shiva: I feel more grounded.

Shakti: Shakti: That is my job.

Shiva: Shiva: But you do it so well

Shakti: You've got it backward: The way I do it is the definition of doing it well.

Shiva: (Smiles) You *are* Divine.

Shakti: As I was saying.

Shiva: Sounds like you are in the mood for more explication.

Shakti: As much as I will ever be. Hit me up.

Shiva: Well, what I was saying was about our being Divine.

Shakti: What do you mean?

Shiva: The relationship between the human world and ours…

Shakti: Far from clear to me….I'd love for you to throw a little light on it.

Shiva: That is my job, and I am delighted to oblige: First off, they say we don't exist.

Shakti: Who says that?

Shiva: Humans.

Shakti: They really say that?

Shiva: Yep.

Shakti: That's pretty cheeky.

Shiva: Well, they've never lacked for arrogance.

Shakti: Look who's talking.

Shiva: All right. I'm not going argue with that.

Shakti: How many humans say that?

Shiva: That we don't exist? A lot. Mostly those outside India.

Shakti: But even if they don't call us "Shiva" and "Shakti," they must know we exist. We're right there inside of them.

Shiva: That's the problem. They're mostly pretty out of touch with what is inside of them.

Shakti: Oh.

Shiva: The good news is a lot of them are beginning to look inside – I think it has to do with having made such a mess of the outside. (Shrugs) Anyhow, whatever works. But they are more and more sitting quietly – "meditation," in English – and looking inwardly.

> *A man returns to himself*
> *When he awakens from sleep;*
> *Likewise, I have perceived the God and Goddess*
> *By waking from my ego.*
>
> — Jnaneshvar

If they persist in that, I don't see how they can miss us....which brings me to our current theme: the different "realities" that a human encounters during the inward journey, and where along the way *we* "live."

Shakti: I'd love it if you shed some of your famous light on that.

Shiva: Well, operationally, for the human mind, moving inward as she sits quietly, after disengaging from the outer world – if she can manage that – she will encounter another space or "reality" which is made up of visual images, archetypal figures, dream-like sequences. Though it can get cluttered with lots of stuff brought along from the outside world, if she sits long and patiently enough, the outlines begin to emerge of this other world. In Sanskrit it's called *taijasa* – the world of primal entities—that spawns and gives shape to the outer world in which humanity lives.

Shakti: How does it shape the outer world?

Shiva: I was afraid that you were going to ask me that. It's hard to explain. Maybe for humans it's most useful to say how it *doesn't* work. In other words, most folks on Earth assume that something appears because it is fabricated – like in a factory – a very materialistic, mechanistic concept. I take these materials and combine them in such and such a way, and I produce an object. This way of thinking carries over into how they assume the world around them and those who inhabit it come into being.

But it ain't necessarily so. You and I are familiar with other realities, and can grasp that the mechanistic version of *causality* is the exception rather than the rule. It is the way material things are reshaped and rearranged "to make something new." But it isn't *new* in the way that a newborn baby is.

Shakti: I agree it's different. But *how* is it different? Or *why* is it different?

Shiva: Because it's not a creation in the sense that that word is understood in English. It's more an emergence out of the seed of another level of being.

Shakti: I have no idea what you are saying.

Shiva: OK, like you and I are the seeds out of which spring the Masculine and Feminine aspects of each person on Earth.

Shakti: Thank you. That's much better. That's something I have experienced – felt....

Shiva: Humans might have a bit more trouble with it.

Shakti: Probably. But you mentioned "different realities" so I assume you were going to specify more than just these two. I want to hear the rest.

Shiva: So what I was just talking about has been called "the mythical" – not because its existence is a myth, as humans would generally have it, but because it is where the stories live that shape us.

Shakti: Shakti: You mean they "shape us" as in being our point of origin, or that they "shape us" in an ongoing way?

Shiva: More the ongoing way – origin is deeper. Ever notice when a person is listening to a story with rapt attention? Their eyes glaze over – they have clearly entered what humans call "an altered state of consciousness." Trouble with that term is that it implies that their everyday waking consciousness is reality with a capital "R." The *real* reality. Anything else is an "altered" state. Of course to us, who are accustomed to traversing realities like humans do neighborhoods, it sounds rather small-minded.

When they enter that state, they are actually shifting into the mythical structure [*] of consciousness. And the story they hear is very likely reconfiguring their mythical reality.

Shakti: Makes me shudder to think what's happening when they flock to the cinema, or worse sit for hours in front of their televisions, watching trashy movies.

Shiva: Now, now. Let's focus on the possibility that they will get their fill, tire of it, and begin to see exactly how having their stories restructured is affecting them.

Shakti: Is that optimistic?

Shiva: Maybe, but only if there's no waking up happening. And I think there is.

Shakti: So what's the next consciousness structure. Aren't there more?

Shiva: Yes, definitely. Deeper than this dreamspace. the mythical, or behind it, or at a higher frequency – however you want to think of it—is the realm of light, energy, largely formless, image-free swirls and streamings. That has been termed *prajna* in Sanskrit (pra, first, and jna, knowledge) or, in English [**] the *magic* structure of consciousness. Again, magic not because it is unreal (the choice of these terms bears witness to the poverty of words available in English to designate subtle phenomena), but because it is the realm where consciousness can *make* [***] things happen through intention and non physical action.

[*]   The term *structure* here is taken from the writings of Jean Gebser (See Bibliography) a Western philosopher who wrote an influential text on the nature of consciousness. It denotes a "reality," in this case, one that is distinct from the one we inhabit routinely – which Gebser terms the *mental*. He also speaks of the *magic* structure, and the *integral*, as well as the *archaic* – the latter which he equates with "source" or *Ursprung*. (See also Glossary and Indexed pages 213.)

[**] See Jean Gebser, Though Gebser was not very familiar with Eastern thought, he ended up reaching many of the same insights that are present in those traditions by pooling the cumulative wisdom of European philosophers, scientists, psychologists and artists.

[***] Gebser uses this term based on his suggestion that the words "make" and "magic" are related through a common Indo-Euopean root ,*mag(h)*-

Shakti: You sort of said that you and I live in the "mythical." But we also live in this space too, what you're calling the "magic," right? I mean, I do—if it's the realm of energy—my name, "shakti," *means* energy.

Shiva: Of course, you're right. Our existence extends into the realm of energy and light...though it is primarily in the mythical where humans experience us.

Shakti: Doesn't the existence of humans extend there, too?

Shiva: Yes, but they are not conscious of it. Their focus is so fixed on their grosser physical nature....

Shakti: Can't that change?

Shiva: Sure, and when it does, they sort of morph into subtler beings – what we would call siddhas, or they might call shamans...

Shakti: So why must these realms be inhabited so separately by different ones of us. You know that I'm a fan of inclusivity.

Shiva: Good point. It's only the attachment to a limited identity—or "ego" which is another word for the same thing – that blocks humans from being more inclusive of all these inner realms. In other words, their self-concept is so limited, that they can only inhabit one—and one designed to be limited enough so that they *can* handle it [*].

Shakti: Can't we help?

Shiva: I'm not sure there's much we can do....They have to get bored [**] with the ego stuff.

Shakti: What happens then?

Shiva: They get curious and start venturing beyond their limited reality.

Shakti: Is it really that simple? Just waiting for them to get fed up with their

---

[*] As explained by Rev. Vyana Bergen: We go into the mythical and magic unconsciously in sleep; to bring them into discussion and articulation feels to us like a violation of an ego boundary.

[**] Certainly there is undeniable pain and suffering caused by living in the thrall of the ego. But ultimately the quality of the disillusionment that leads to change might be aptly described as a sort of boredom (or ennui, as the French existentialists liked to call it in the mid-twentieth century).

nonsense. Isn't that sort of like Nero fiddling while Rome burns? If I have my human history straight...

Shiva: Yes...it does take time – but we have plenty of that – remember that time we were having sex for a thousand years and all the other gods were waiting for us to conceive Skanda....

Shakti: Yeah, but time for them – for humans—is different. They have themselves caught in a time trap.

Shiva: I hear your concern, but isn't this a little trick of your own....After all Kali means literally "time". And She is known to use time to humble the stubborn ego with the ravages of age.

Shakti: Well, I've had to do that. They just weren't getting with the program. It's gentler than lopping off heads, isn't it?

Shiva: Yes, dear. Maybe not as effective, though. And in the long run, can you really say there is less suffering – or could there even be more...

Shakti: Why sometimes I think you might be egging me on...I mean me as Kali...

Shiva: I'll leave the timing to Her.....I'm sure you know better than me, but I get the sense that she's getting ready to rise up....

Shakti: What other recourse do we have?

Shiva: Well, it's ultimately about the marriage. The union of Masculine and Feminine that will open the 3rd eye [*]....Humans need to be curious enough to at least explore that possibility – the union. But we know that that is also nudged along by our dialogue here, the more we understand each other, the more we enter into this union ourselves, and then the more they are prompted to do so within themselves...

Shakti: So it all comes back to the marriage. That's fine with me. I'm delighted to make conversation and love with you indefinitely. But my Yin Feminine side does feel for the human dilemma, and my Kali is appropriately impatient when they don't move along developmentally....

[*]   In traditional yogic terms the opening of sushumna

Shiva: And there will be no marriage if Kali is not included. I mean you and I cannot really come to union if I don't accept the Kali side of you. And humans can't have an inner marriage until they accept their own Yang Feminine, i.e., their own shakti and *their own Kali.* Maybe they will never do that without Her showing up to shake things loose on a large scale. They may need to see that happen and then also see that it forces them into the changes they had needed to make to find more happiness and joy. Maybe that's what it will take for them to come to really love Her ,the way that I have.

Shakti: I'm touched. (Shiva looks at her skeptically)....No, really! But I have one more question: What exactly happens to humans when the Third Eye opens?

Shiva: Then the Structures of Consciousness we talked about are all in the human's awareness. She/he is aware of the everyday mundane world (the Mental), the Mythical world and the Magic – as well as the Origin from which it all emerges. But not aware of them in sequence as now happens—one during the day, then that is blotted out, and there is only awareness of one of the others during one phase of sleep, then that's lost, and another moves into awareness—that sort of serial schizophrenia. Instead, it's as though you can see them all as transparent overlays, one on top of the other. What that is, is a completely new Structure of Consciousness, another, broader,—and you will be glad to hear – more *inclusive* consciousness that is now often being called the Integral.

Shakti: Sort of like us!

Shiva: Exactly. To be more specific, a consciousness that moves beyond time, space and causality.

Shakti: They become gods.

Shiva: Well, something close to that.

Shakti: Shakti: I can't wait to see it happen. But it could get crowded up here.

Shiva: You know better than that. It's *beyond time, space....*

Shakti: I'm only teasing you....

FOUNDATIONAL MEDITATION 2

Masculine and Feminine Currents

As in the first Meditation on Breath practice, establish your posture and then run through a systematic relaxation, so that any unnecessary muscular exertion is eliminated and you can focus your attention on your breath.

Again, begin your breath awareness with a minute or so of observing your current breathing pattern.

Now turn your attention to the sensation of the breath in your nostrils. This is a sensation that is going on unceasingly, so it is usually one that we have learned to ignore. In order to bring it fully into awareness, see if you can notice the difference between the warmth of the stream of outgoing air and the coolness of the incoming stream. In what parts of your nasal passageways do you feel this? Where is it most pronounced?

Now see if you can determine through which nostril the largest volumn of air is flowing. Right or Left [*]? Choose the nostril that is more noticeably open, and look at how that is related to your body image at this moment:

Is that side of your body more or less vivid to you? Is it larger or smaller? Brighter or darker? Which side feels more open and fluid? Which feels more tight and constricted. Which heavier; which lighter?

Now attend to the nostril that was most closed, the one where the sensation is less and where the airflow seems less. As you do so, notice the sensation of the air passing over the various nooks and crannies of the inner space of that nostril. Focus on the coolness of the air being inhaled and the warmth of the air being exhaled. Imagine that side of your body growing larger, brighter, more active. After a minute or so, you may notice that the volume of air moving through this nostril – the one you are now scrutinizing—has increased.

Now remember that the right side is connected to your Masculine, the left to your Feminine. Which, then, is more prominent in your awareness and functioning at this moment? Can you notice a different flavor, a different sense of self, a different inclination to act in ways that are more typical of your Masculine (or Feminine) with each nostril's opening or "activation?" Experiment with this for a few minutes.

[*]   If this all seems inaccessible to you, you might wish to explore the yogic practice of Alternate Nostril Breathing (nadi shodhanam). See, e.g., *The Science of Breath*, Himalayan Institute Press.

PRINCIPLES 5 & 6

as elucidated by Lord Shiva for his Divine Consort, Shakti

Principle 5. *The marriage is also of the ascending current with the descending.*

Shiva: Up to now, we've been talking primarily about the union of left and right – as you and I are depicted in the image of the Ardharanishvara, the "half and half god" – uh, or *deity*.

Shakti: Thank you....

Shiva: But there is another aspect of the marriage. That is the marriage of the ascending power – you – and the descending light – me.

Shakti: How's that different?

Shiva: Because of the process. The light descends, and in doing so, brings awareness to each chakra it illuminates.

Shakti: How is that done?

Shiva: It's part of the meditation experience. I mean it can happen through life experience, too. A young man, or woman for that matter, learning martial arts is usually working intensely with the Third Chakra – becoming more aware of his or her aggression, how he or she responds to aggression from another, and establishing mastery of the body and its capacity to act and protect itself. Where this awareness is received, I am bringing the light of consciousness.

Shakti: So this is a sequential process: chakra five, four, three, etc?

Shiva: Not necessarily, though there is some tendency to work ones way in a generally downward direction.

Shakti: Why?

Shiva: Because the further you go down the more primitive and challenging are the energies and issues you encounter.

Shakti: You know I don't like that word "primitive" – especially when applied to my home territory – the lower three charkas...

Shiva: Right. How about "primal"?

Shakti: I like that much better – it has the flavor of "primary." Which is appropriate, I think. That energy "down there," like the earth itself, is the wellspring of life on this plane...

Shiva: Hence the importance of the descent reaching all the way down. As each chakra is illumined by the light of consciousness, it automatically begins to undergo some reconfiguration.

Shakti: Why would that happen automatically?

Shiva: Because when the feelings, memories, impulses, and conflicts held in that center are brought into fuller consciousness they begin to be compared to and revised by that new and more inclusive consciousness.

Shakti: It sounds like you are saying that, for example, if there are apparent contradictions, then something is adjusted to bring it into agreement with the rest.

Shiva: Could be.

Shakti: But what about the utility of letting contradictory statements coexist – of accepting inconsistencies. "A foolish consistency is the hobgoblin of little minds." Wasn't that what you mentioned?

Shiva: OK, I am hearing you. And I am aware that hyper-rational thinking is limiting. I'm not talking about bringing everything into rigid agreement. I'm more saying that by having different aspects of yourself consciously juxtaposed, you change. It's like the power of diversity in community.

Shakti: I'm not sure I follow that last part, but it feels true.

Shiva: So bringing the light of consciousness down to lower chakras necessarily reprograms those above.

Shakti: I believe that. But tell me how you see it happening. Can you give me an example?

Shiva: Sure. One may feel he has an "open heart" and a basically compassionate stance in the world, but still distance him from heavy-duty criminals – like murderers or rapists – in subtle but palpable ways. After exploring one's own lower charkas and getting in touch with a bit of the blind rage or whatever had been hidden there, there is a whole different level of acceptance and love for those who have transgressed [*].

---

[*]   There are various steps and processes involved here. For example bringing light (consciousness) to the "content" of the lower chakra, the release of the energy required that had been being used to keep it unconscious, and the use of that energy to further "open" (activate) the higher chakra. There are also techniques for "releasing" the retired content of the lower chakra that is no longer being "used." For the latter one might use a cleansing breath, an exaggeration of apana vayu (as described in *Chapt 10 of Radical Healing*), or mantras such as the Gayatri Mantra.

Shakti: All right. I am totally with you now. I'd put it more bluntly: all the "stuff" in the lower three chakras has to be integrated or the opening of the heart is fake.

Shiva: The same can been said about the inner marriage – our marriage [*] – and the opening of the third eye. If there is unconscious stuff bubbling and roiling in the lower chakras, this also grossly colors and distorts the possibility of true union.

Shakti: You talk about that in the conditional, but isn't that exactly what is happening wholesale now in the world: that this great mass evolutionary step of moving into a totally new way of being on the planet is sabotaged by all the unconscious violence that runs through everything that humans do?

Shiva: Very well said! My, my. Are you angling for my job?

Shakti: (Coyly) Of course not. I just wanted to be sure that I understand what you are revealing to me.

Shiva: Guardedly) Uh huh......

Shakti: But I have another question. You talked about the marriage as happening in the heart, now you're back to the third eye – i.e., the pineal/ Sixth Chakra. Which is it?

Shiva: (Recovering his poise) You might say that the heart is where the wedding ceremony takes place. The temple shaped to capture the essence of the union. It has four chambers: two feminine on the left – one receptive and one active. And there are two masculine on the right – one active and one receptive. We might see the heart as a four chambered hall where each aspect of the union is celebrated, or we might see it as a piece of sacred, living, sculptural art – an installation – designed to bring to life the four fold function of the integrated being. If such a piece were in a museum, we can imagine standing before it for hours, awed by its complexity and symmetry.

Shakti: That's beautiful. And the Ajna Chakra – the Third Eye/I?

[*] Shiva here is emphasizing that the inner marriage is the marriage of Shakti and Him. It is also true that their marriage, that of Shiva and Shakti, has parallels in the outer world – stretching into the cosmos.

Shiva: Well, if the heart is the wedding chapel, then the Ajna Chakra – the *deep* aspect of it in the interior of the skull – in the area of the pineal gland, is where the married couple goes to live. Where they live in bliss, happily ever after except, of course, that is now a meaningless expression, since they dwell beyond time space and causality.

Shakti: Whew! That's nice to understand, but I think I really enjoyed grasping it by living through the process – rather than hearing it described and explained....

Shiva: But you did ask.

Shakti: I know. And you answered beautifully.

Shiva: So....

Shakti: You're about to put this topic to bed now and move on aren't you?

Shiva: Yes...

Shakti: Well, there are a few things I need to clear up.

Shiva: Go ahead.

Shakti: A few things you made reference to, but didn't explain.

Shiva: OK.

Shakti: You mentioned the ego and it's relationship to limited reality. Why is that so – why does it imply or result in a limited reality?

Shiva: Because when you limit the world to what you can imagine/envision that becomes your reality.
   It's like leading with your butt – the least knowledgeable part of yourself....

Shakti: Hold on. I'd argue that what you "know" in your Root Chakra is more significant than all that in your head.

Shiva: You think I'll never learn?

Shakti: No, I just think you need to be reminded....

Shiva: It's an appropriate correction. Actually leading with your head is more accurate if we're talking about the ego. It just doesn't have the same dramatic value as a figure of speech. Anyway, you get the point.

Shakti: I think so. You also mentioned my Kali strategies to use time to counter the ego. But I wanted to hear more about ageing and its value. It's part of Nature's plan, in any case, which means I am, on some deep level on the same page with it.

Shiva: Humans have lots of "living out" of their issues to do during the course of their lives. That takes up decades of a life and amounts to a sort of clearing – often by the last stage of their time on Earth they can allow us – you and me—to come through more clearly.... It amounts to a kind of "pay-off."

This especially true when it comes to letting the Yang Feminine express – call it your Kali energy. This is probably accurately termed "coming into your power," something that is very much needed on the planet now.

Unfortunately most old people are captured, drugged, and locked away – cash cows for the pharmaceutical houses.

Shakti: You're exaggerating.

Shiva: Maybe a little. But basically it's true. Anyway, what they might be saying at this point is effectively squelched. It surely amounts to another strategy for purging Kali from the land – whether it's done consciously or not.

Shakti: This seems to me like the result of a health problem. I mean the general disregard of humans for the piece of Gaia they have been most intimately entrusted with – their bodies.

Shiva: That's right on the mark. The tragedy is that they get caught in a vicious circle. If their bodies are not in good working order, their consciousness becomes clouded. Then they are even less likely to realize that they are abusing and neglecting their bodies. The classic exploitation of the Feminine sets in, where they – women as well as men – adopt the typical twisted version of the Masculine: I'm hungry, where's my food? They expect the body to pump nourishment around to all their cells, whether they have cared for it or not. Or: I want to go do things, quit complaining and nagging: The body should take me where I want to go, function as an instrument and vehicle for my schemes whether it's had rest or not [*]. And so on…. Eventually Kali pulls off one of her extreme interventions: She burns the house down.

Shakti: You mean….er…ends the life?

Shiva: Exactly. I guess the logic is, if you're not going to get with the program, but instead abuse your body indefinitely, then this is a dead end, and we might as well call it a game and deal a new hand…

Shakti: Which might look an awful lot like the previous hand.

Shiva: Unfortunately.

Shakti: Are we ending this section.

Shiva: Yes

Shakti: Is that a sour note to end on?

Shiva: Not if it's a tribute to Kali – and leading ultimately to a juicy discussion of pleasure!

Shakti: In that case…

---

[*] This perspective on physical health is elaborated and clarified in *Part II Chapter 1*.

Principle 6. *Another perspective on the path*
of Tantra focuses on how the rise of (Kundalini)
Shakti activates the chakras

Shiva: Another way of understanding transformation is to look at another aspect of what is happening during the process. Traditionally that is spoken of as the rise of kundalini shakti.

Shakti: Does it strike you as a bit strange that you are describing kundalini shakti to me, when I *am* Shakti?

Shiva: (mildly offended) Not at all! You are shakti, I am that which elucidates it. What's your problem?

Shakti: (chastened) Well, nothing really....It just seemed odd.....But I hear you....I guess there is a difference between my *being* and your *seeing*, but why can't everyone do both.

Shiva: So much talk about humans has made you think you are one! Indeed, that is what we are aiming for here, that humans allow you and me to become as one within them: the inner marriage of the masculine principle and the feminine principle. Our job after all, is to demonstrate exactly who those two marriage partners are, and how they reach a state of union. And that can't happen until humans are clear about what the Masculine and Feminine really are, until their distortions of them are stripped away. We stand for the universal clarification of the masculine principle and the feminine one. Our very existence is meant to provide clear and easily grasped prototypes for the two.

Shakti: I see. That makes sense. But there is nothing wrong with the longing to integrate it all into one...

Shiva: Of course not. In fact, that is the longing that is being felt all over planet Earth. It is the longing that will fuel the inner marriage and lead to the opening of the Sixth Chakra – the Third Eye/I. In the meantime, you can even see that longing expressed in the fading of gender lines – especially among young people. It's creating quite a bit of havoc in the external marriage, too, incidentally....not to mention with gender roles in the workplace. The chaos of transformation.... your Kali at work, no doubt.

Shakti: Let me get something straight here. So who is getting called Kali here, who shakti and who kundalini? If I listen to too much of that I will begin to feel like I have a multiple personality disorder...

Shiva: It's really all just linguistic attempts to get a fix on your multifaceted magnificence! And it's all about energy and power—what you are. Shakti is the generic term for your power which is found not only in the human, but all through nature and the universe. Kundalini refers to the particular quantum of shakti that is the individual human's to work with and is usually concentrated in the pelvic bowl – or *kunda*. And of course, Kali is your own one-woman cosmic hit squad. [*]

But our subject of the moment is the kundalini – or kundalini shakti, as it is more precisely labeled. One aspect of personal transformation – one that caught the attention of the yogis – was that when transformation is really on a roll, you can feel the jolts of energy moving up from the pelvic bowl along the spine. And when that happens, you can notice that the chakras along the path of the rising kundalini are activated, often dramatically.

Shakti: And what is the effect of that....I mean what can you notice?

Shiva: Well, to answer that, we will need to remember the nature of Kundalini's fall and rescue. Why she is said to be asleep, intoxicated, coiled between the first and second chakras (i.e., between the anal center and the genital one). Now, kundalini also means serpent. So she is a serpent that uncoils and, hissing loudly, ascends along the spine, until she reaches the crown of the head and enlightenment ensues.

That, of course, is a rather dramatic and sudden version of the process. More often it is a step-wise affair, with increments of the shakti becoming available at each step of progress.

Shakti: And how does she manage to come out of her stupor and rise?

Shiva: Well, there's another little description of that. In this version, the serpent is a lovely young damsel. She is however, in sad shape, lying drunk between the first and second chakras, in the gutter, so to speak. She is disheveled, besmirched, bedraggled, and only intermittently semi-conscious. At that point, when things are looking pretty hopeless for her, along comes a kindly and handsome young man, who stops and is touched by her situation and her still visible beauty. He gently awakens her, helps her to her feet and takes her to her home. There she recovers her strength, cleans herself up, dresses herself up as the goddess she is, and from there rises in Her glory.

[*] It should be clarified here that this is only one of the many ways that these goddesses are conceived in the vast, rich, and varied Indic traditions. In Kerala, for example, Kali is often thought of as having two distinct guises: one nurturing, caring, and kind, the other vengeful, frightening, and dangerous. The various functions of the Feminine are thus represented singly or in combinations as local custom dictates.

The young man was Tapas. The place he took her was the Second Chakra, whose Sanskrit name is Svadisthana, literally, "her true home."

Shakti: So it was tapas that did the trick.

Shiva: Yes. The use of the technique of tapas allowed the breaking of the habits that kept her there.

Shakti: And how did habits keep her between the first and second chakras?

Shiva: There were habits of consumption, for example, that did it: the urge to acquire more things, or to eat more—or whatever—to fill the void that comes from fear of death. The first chakra has to do with survival – the fears that surround that – fears of annihilation, for example. When there is total identification with the physical body, then one is terrified of losing it. And of course, it is going to go at some point. Therefore reason only confirms the terror. So her energy can't get from the first chakra preoccupation with survival of the self. It can't even rise to the second, genital, chakra, which is, (at least biologically), preoccupied with the survival of the species.

Shakti: So that's why she's "drunk"—no shakti to power her life because it's all drained away into the acquisitions addiction and other strategies to stave off visions of the Grim Reaper.

Shiva: Precisely.

Shakti: And why is the Second Chakra "her true home?" I mean, I'm actually asking, aren't I, why it's *my* true home? Or is that what you are saying?

Shiva: Yes, that is what I'm saying. It is her and your true home, because, first off, it's the initial step in the movement of energy up the ladder of chakras, to get beyond pure self-interest and self-preoccupation. As long as you are concerned with survival, it's hard to be interested in anything else. Second, this chakra, the Genital, is the center from where this human quantum of power can be moved and expressed. Though reproduction gets the first shot at it – to ensure perpetuation of the bloodline and of the species – it has much more interesting uses.

Shakti: Like?

Shiva: Like moving up the spine to switch on one chakra after another.

Hence she comes home, bedecks herself, and "rises in her glory."

Shakti: I think you still haven't answered my question about what one can notice when those chakras are being activated as she "rises."

Shiva: Sorry. Well, if she gets to the second chakra, you got a lot more sexual energy. That's not difficult to notice. If more shakti moves into the Third Chakra, the Solar Plexus or Manipura, you may become more assertive, certainly issues of power and surrender and mastery capture your attention more readily. Digestion improves, and there's more warmth in the belly and in the body in general. As if the stove was stoked.

Shakti: Ah! That's the kind of explanation I like. Embodied, in the best sense of the word.

Shiva: Of course, the heart opening is well recognized: compassion, desire to nurture, connection – as well as a stronger physical heart. Usually an opening of the chest: it expands more, when it has been so protected by your shoulders, for example.

Shakti: I'm remembering you said something earlier about chakras getting reconfigured as others are activated….what was that?

Shiva: As the Solar Plexus (which is to say the third) Chakra is amped up, and you experience more sense of mastery and confidence, and more physical vitality, then your sexual expression – one chakra down, the second—becomes less inhibited, more dynamic. As that happens, and it, the second, is more open and less conflicted, then energy can flow through it more readily, and the third gets even more activated.

And the same process occurs with the relation between the 3rd and 4th: as the third is more active, it allows energy up to the heart (the fourth chakra), and the heart, opening more allows you to revise how you see Third Chakra issues of control, mastery, and dominance. You begin to realize that there are ways that dominance can be used lovingly, rather than for exploitation. Asserting authority with an employee can, when done at just the right moment, support them in curbing their distractibility, or help them show up on time and gain more self-confidence as a result.

So you might picture the whole process as a series of circling whirls of energy, light, and activation [see diagram] that can gain momentum and eventually sweep up the spine, bringing into play a chain reaction of reconfigurations, and leaving in its wake a transformed pathway for shakti to rise through.

Shakti: So are you saying that the more this kind of inner storm of transformation can be set in motion, the less I need to marshal an outer Kali storm of rectifying devastation to jar things back on track?

Shiva: Exactly. It's only the inattentiveness and resistance to transformation that has put the planet so far out of step with the natural flow of change. Enough people reigniting the fires of transformation within themselves can bump us ahead enough that you won't have to clean house and start all over.

Shakti: How do we sell this?

Shiva: That's easy. Sex.

Shakti: Excuse me?

Shiva: Sex and pleasure, which are the topics of our next and final tantric principle.

Shakti: Now this is getting really interesting!

FOUNDATIONAL MEDITATION 3

The Breath of Union

As in the first two Meditations on Breath:
1. Establish your posture
2. Do a systematic relaxation, and
3. Spend a few moments in an initial observation of your breath

Now, bring your attention to the point between the nostrils.

Focus there, where the nasal septum intersects the upper lip. Concentrate on the precise point that is at the center of that area. Notice the flow of cool air entering the nostrils on each side, then the flow of warm air leaving on each side of that precise point.

After a few minutes of this concentration, you will probably notice that the breath has moved toward equilibrium – with more nearly equal flow on the two sides. Once that has happened, begin to follow the course of the flow from the point between the nostrils upward toward the point between the eyebrows. On each breath follow it a bit higher until you are able to stay with it all the way up from the point between the two nostrils to the point between the eyebrows. Continue with several breaths that run the full course, connecting these two points. Once you are able to do this, you may then allow your attention to rest on the point between the eyebrows.

See if you can notice the change in the quality of your awareness as you settle into this point.

If you have trouble with the equalization of the breath, simply stay with that step for the duration of the present session. Steadying your focus is a valuable skill to develop. After some days of this, the breath will begin to settle more readily into a flow that is equal on the two sides.

This equal flow, the *sushumna* of the yogis, reflects a bilateral activation of the two hemispheres of the brain. It is the sort of state that one enters during hypnotic trance. This is a perfect mode of function for meditation: it is not a good foundation for action in the world. Engagement with your surroundings is best undertaken when you are in the right nostril – for active engagement (what we have termed the Masculine). Or the left – for more receptive engagement (the Feminine).

Ideally, this exercise will provide you some opportunity to become more consciously acquainted with your capacity to function in these two modes, as well as the difference that marks the Union of the Two (the foundation of the Inner Marriage).

PRINCIPLE 7

as elucidated by Lord Shiva for his Divine Consort, Shakti

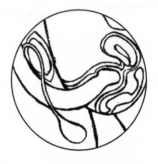

Principle 7. *Pleasure is at the heart of the tantric path,*
it has the capacity to heal, and is closely identified
with its corollary, play.

Shakti: Is this something new? You've never said anything like this in previous tantras.

Shiva: No, it's not really new. It was just implicit before. There was no need to say it….Sort of like the discussion of tapas. That is usually taken for granted, too. All our Indic devotees to the tantric path know that tapas is an essential part of the practice. It's woven into their upbringing, their education and their lives…

Shakti: As is the essential role of pleasure.

Shiva: Right.

Shakti: I do find it annoying that you always say "right" and never "left."

Shiva: I mean, really. What kind of objection is that……I know: right is the masculine side and left is the feminine, but it's the *language*.

Shakti: I know that. But don't try to trivialize what I'm saying. And it's not a tangential objection. It's actually related to what you were just talking about.

Shiva: What do you mean?

Shakti: Well, you were apparently setting out to take issue with some of the cultural biases that have entered the discussion of Tantra from the West.

Shiva: Ri….uh…correct…

Shakti: And those biases extend into the very language that we are using. Not just English, either. The whole Indo-European branch of the family: Latin into Italian, for example. The left side is *sinestra*, whence the English word, sinister – hardly conveying respect and honor to Her – She who resides on the "left." I hate to stoop to one of your puns, but that's all she gets: what's *left*.

Shiva: OK. I do see what you are saying now. I want to say that it seems like a small matter, but I know you'll take issue with that….

Shakti: (her voice rising) I will indeed. I'm trying to broaden the discussion you began. (Catching herself, and dropping to a lighter tone) And if you call me a "broad," I swear I will call down the wrath of Kali on you!

Shiva: (rolls his eyes at the corny pun) That's beneath even me.

Shakti: But, seriously, let's not just pay lip service to ferreting out the biases in the language and culture. Let's be thorough about it: for there are a lot. The misogyny runs through fore to aft and starboard to f'castle – or whatever it is that they say.

Shiva: You are correct. And the subtle condemnation of pleasure is only one of the misogynistic tendencies that permeate the entire world-view of that Euro American/Anglo Indian culture. While it may not overtly connect pleasure to the feminine, it must sense the connection – surely the physiology of the human body strongly suggests it: The clitoris has more (four times as many) nerve endings to register pleasure than the penis, despite its size…

Shakti: She – I – is/am designed to experience pleasure. Gaia, the earth, is a paradise – a pleasure generator! Pleasure is the overflow she pours over the universe to nourish its life. Without pleasure, everything dries up, shrivels.

("Life is but voluptuousness." Kamalakar Mishra)

Shiva: And at the very heart of the tantric world view is pleasure, play, and dance. That is why I am often depicted dancing.

Shakti: I love those dancing statues of you!

Shiva: (smiles) They are nice, aren't they?
But it seems the modern – or is it the modern western? – mind finds it difficult to imagine a spiritual path that is based on *play*. Somehow to qualify as spiritual it must be grim, solemn, judgmental, and a bit rigid. Dancing and sexuality are "inappropriate."

Shakti: I can't really understand the attraction that sort of approach holds for humans.

Shiva: Well, it certainly came in on the coattails of the British – and to some extent the Moguls before them. The best the English language could do with the Latin root word *ludic*, which means "having to do with play," is their word "ludicrous" with its connotation of absurd, ridiculous—certainly not worthy of being the distinguishing qualifier of a path to spiritual attainment.

* * *

Prem Saran, author and anthropologist, who grew up in India, relates his difficulty as a youth in grasping the anhedonic attitude of western spirituality:

"I went to a ... school...run by Catholic priests, of whom a few were European; I studied there until I matriculated at 16. It was a good school, and the good Fathers made no conscious attempt to indoctrinate their non-Christian wards...

Still, I could not help imbibing some core elements of the Judaeo-Christian weltanschaung, especially in its Western form....

I learnt about the shame of nudity, linked as it was with the irrevocable Fall of humanity; the iniquity of man's Original Sin; the essential and fatal moral weakness of Eve; the Serpent and the dangers of unsupervised and thus illicit knowledge, sensual and other; the awful goodness of God and the incorrigible wickedness of Satan; the total 'otherness' of deity and of the sacred; the need to confess one's transgressions and succumbed temptations to authority figures, as per the Lord's Prayer. I also learned about Jesus and his Immaculate conception by an all-good Virgin; how He suffered the most painful torture to save us for our sins; how He resurrected in the flesh, and has promised us the same on the Day of Last Judgment, provided we are good; the need to believe and repent for our sins; the need to open ourselves to God's grace, or face the torments of the damned in Hell....

I also did learn somewhat later in life about the more attractive portions of this fire-and brimstone religious ideology: Psalm 23, the Sermon on the Mount, the Songs of Solomon, Gregorian chants, and so on. But the overall impression is of a world view that, at least in its unalloyed Western incarnations, inculcates extremely radical social-psychological splits between: man and woman, man and deity, man and animal; man and nature; body and mind; sensual and spiritual experience; good and evil; sacred and profane; conscious and unconscious; Western and non-Western man; and so on....."

Prem Saran P 6

* * *

Shakti: How did Tantra survive that?

Shiva: One might say that it only survived in its ludic fullness where the Moguls and the British invasions penetrated the least: Kerala in the far south, Bengal and Assam to the extreme East, and Nepal to the north.

Like the whole left/right language thing, the deprecation of the ludic is the banishment of *spanda*. Spanda is play – it is the play of the life force. Restrain it and there is no real play. All this is related to the attempt to deny the existence of the yang feminine.

Shakti: Why is she so feared and hated?

Shiva: As we have seen before, it is the need to control....to protect the interests of the ego and to avoid the unpredictable. Therefore: no spontaneity, no play, no pleasure. Only then can you eliminate spanda and
her terrifying alter ego, Kali. Of course, the irony is that the longer
you suppress spanda, the more likely you are to rouse Kali! She will
not be denied.

Shakti: So pleasure is not just one of the tantric principles, it runs through others.

Shiva: Through all of them. I would think that you would know that.

Shakti: I just wanted to hear you say it.

Shiva: OK. I will: it runs through "everything is an experiment," spanda,
and even tapas.

Shakti: How tapas? That's prototypically masculine – testicular, in fact!

Shiva: True. But tapas properly done has an experimental quality to it: I
am going to contain this habit, and see what happens." I really don't
know exactly what will happen, because I merely refuse to allow the
energy to flow into the habit and wait for spanda to take over. When
it does, some creative, delightful surprise arises. In fact, I'm playing –
playing for the pleasure of seeing what emerges!

Shakti: It's our working together at its best.

Shiva: Delightful.

Shakti: And the other principles?

Shiva: Well, the inner marriage is all about the bliss of union. The pleasure
there is almost indescribable.
   In fact, the ascent of kundalini, with the successive activation of
the chakras, at each step results in a more subtle and exquisite pleasure.

Shakti: It begins to sound suspiciously abstract.

Shiva: How so?

Shakti: I just want to point out that it cannot be disembodied – even though
it is going to higher and subtler chakras. Remember your whirl and
swirl visual of the movement up and then back down the chakras?

Even though the focus of the activation may be another chakra up, there's the spin off reconfiguration of the ones below it, and this is resonating and vibrating in your whole being, including the lowest chakras, that is, *if* the rising of Kundalini – me – is the real thing, and not just a useless head trip or a stoner's mind fuck.

Shiva: Strong language.

Shakti: Important point.

Shiva: Agreed. The lower chakras become re configured, experience fuller pleasure, and are not "transcended."

Shakti: That's it, that's what I was trying to say.

Shiva: So, ultimately, throughout the exploration of these tantric principles, the quest for deeper and subtler pleasure causes you to go to more refined and more spiritual heights to find that pleasure. The search for more exquisite pleasure leads you to spirit.

Shakti: I really hate to object again. I know that we are about to end this dialogue, and that it would be really nice if it could end on a cordial note. But there is something here that I can't quite overlook. I mean, I agree with what you are saying as far as the basic content. But there is something about the way you are putting this that makes it sound a lot like a cave in to the western-style moralism police. Like maybe you are part of the Tantra current that wanted to be legitimate, and figured that if I can get the teaching across by throwing a few crumbs to moralism, then why not?

Shiva: Can you be a little more specific?

Shakti: Well, I don't know. I'm not sure that I can. But I can feel the snag in it. It's like pleasure doesn't have to be *justified*. It doesn't need a "higher spiritual purpose" to be OK. It is its own justification. It is at the foundation of the flow of life. We have to able to experience – without apologies – the flow of life as pleasure. Nothing short of that is going to satisfy me.

Shiva: Well, OK, then. Actually, I'm glad you said that. I think it's a perfect note to end on.

[Shakti glows, Shiva dances, and – you know the rest. And if you don't (and want to), do the masculine/feminine meditation (page 97) until you do!]

THE EPILOGUE

Shakti: The what? I thought we were through.

Shiva: This is the evaluation.

Shakti: I never heard of an evaluation in a tantra.

Shiva: It's new.

Shakti: New? But this is a thousand year-old tradition.

Shiva: I know, but it's a necessary update.

Shakti: Why?

Shiva: Because things are changing. I mean, I used to just talk and you pretty much listened.

Shakti: You mean this time it was not just a dialogue in name only.

Shiva: Well....let's just say that in the past there was a fuller separation of the masculine and feminine functions.

Shakti: All right. What do we do?

Shiva: Critique. Do you have any comments to offer?

Shakti: Well....not really. I made them when I needed to. I think it's up to you.

Shiva: I...uh...well, I really felt....I....

Shakti: What are you trying to say?

Shiva: Do you think that maybe you overstepped your role at times?

Shakti: How do you mean?

Shiva Arrogated some of the masculine principle's functions.

Shakti: (annoyed) Arrogated your arrogance?

Shiva: No…but…

Shakti: I thought that we had laid this to rest earlier: I am colored by cultural trends – women consciously accessing their masculine capacities…. and then projecting them onto me as the archetype, so that I begin to morph….

Shiva: But I thought that we also agreed that our job is to clean up the distortions of the pure masculine and pure feminine principles, so that there would be a clearer inner representation of them for the humans to tune in to and call on as they moved toward their inner marriage.

Shakti: True….

Shiva: So don't you have to drop some of that….

Shakti: Drop the vigilance about misogyny and subtle deprecations of Her?

Shiva: Well….yes.

Shakti: My answer is *yes*, I do have to drop them and will have the luxury of doing so when you take them over.

Shiva: Oh….

Shakti: It is your role isn't it? You know…testicular, containment, protection of the space…

Shiva: Uh…yes.

Shakti: (bows sweetly) Then I am at your service, my master, and bear this burden for you faithfully until you lift it from my shoulders.

Shiva: (looks thoughtful, but remains silent)

She/He meditation

This meditation is an opportunity to find the Shiva/Shakti dynamic of the preceding dialogue inside yourself – or, rather, to discover your own variation on it. It is meant to help you embody the understanding you gained from Part I.

If you are a newcomer to meditation, you will find it helpful to go through – or review, if you have already done them—the short preparatory meditations found after each chapter in Part I. This more complex exploration builds on them.

First establish a comfortable seated posture. That is important—crucial for Her to feel that you are acknowledging the importance of embodiment and pleasure. If you can sit cross-legged comfortably, that is ideal, since that helps maintain good blood flow to the brain, so that He can employ full and unimpeded consciousness. An erect posture also promotes opening of sushumna, or equal flow in the two nostrils, which is necessary for the third I/eye to be activated.

When you have established the best posture that is possible today, let it be, and turn your attention to the breath.

First, watch the breath. Notice its rate – is it fast or slow?—then its rhythm. Is it smooth or jerky? Are there pauses or interruptions? At first don't try to alter the breath, simply observe it. Once you have taken stock of your breathing inclinations, you may invite the breath to relax into a regular rhythm. If there were pauses, relax the muscles that restrained the breath during the pause and allow the flow to continue without restraints or interruptions.

Once the posture is established and stable and the breath is regular and relaxed, turn your attention to the point between the nostrils. Focus there, where the nasal septum intersects the upper lip. Concentrate on the precise point that is at the center of that area. Notice the flow of cool air entering the nostrils on each side, then the flow of warm air leaving on each side of that precise point.

After a few minutes of this concentration, you will probably notice that the breath has moved toward equilibrium – with more nearly equal flow on the two sides. Once that has happened, begin to follow the course of the flow from the point between the nostrils upward toward the point between the eyebrows. On each breath follow it a bit higher until you are able to stay with it all the way up from the point between the two nostrils to the point between the eyebrows. Continue with several breaths that run the full course, connecting these two points. Then allow your attention to rest on the point between the eyebrows.

Notice the change in the quality of your awareness as you settle into this point.

After you have enjoyed that for a while, begin to inhale back from that point, following the breath back a little further each time you inhale. Gradually extend this backward course, as though you are allowing yourself to sink back, as you might sink back into a big overstuffed chair.

When you find the point about two or three inches behind the point between the eyebrows, at approximately the center of the skull, allow yourself to rest there. This should put you in the vicinity of the pineal gland—a receptor of light, literally the third eye. This is the "true" Third Eye or Sixth Chakra, and this is where you want to "sit" for the main portion of this meditation.

Settle into your "easy chair" here, and make yourself comfortable.

Once you feel at home here, you may begin to look down toward the right side of your body, allowing your masculine, the He aspect of your inner world to begin to take shape. You may begin to have a sense of what He would look like if He were a separate person. Or you may merely feel sensations in the right side of your body (which is regulated by the left side of the brain and can reflect the emotions, unease, tension, or mood of the masculine aspect of yourself). Or you may experience his mind set, even "imagine" his speaking (if so, go with your imagining, and listen). The form of the glimpses and intuitions about what He has to "say" varies from person to person. Sometimes it's as simple as brief visual impression of a figure – does it feel cowed, angry, depressed? What can you infer from that image? What ever it is, that's fine. Don't try to make something happen, simply tune into what is there.

Once you have perceived whatever there is to "see" (or "hear" or "feel"), shift your attention over to the left side. Now allow Her to take shape. Again, She will reveal herself to you in whatever form She pleases, and all you need to do is remain alert and observant.

Next you move into your role as counselor. From your chair, ask Her gently if she would like to share Her concerns, Her frustrations, Her anxieties, Her challenges, Her agonies. Listen as She "speaks," (or feels, or gestures). Give Her time, inviting Her to share with you, but suggesting that She might like to direct some of Her concerns to Him also.

When you have had enough time to get the general gist of Her concerns and Her feelings, politely ask Her to draw Her sharing to a close, thank Her for Her willingness to reveal Herself to you, and, if you feel that you will wish to do so, assure Her that She will have another time later to express more of what is "on Her mind."

When She has finished, turn your attention back to Him. Now ask Him, in a similar manner to share His concerns, His frustrations, His goals, His apprehensions, His struggles. Again, aiming to encourage dialogue and understanding, suggest that He speak to her as much as he can. Give him your full attention, too. When he has finished, thank him for his courage and his sharing, and, again, if you feel you can realistically do so, tell him you will provide another time to talk in the near future.

Perhaps at this point you would like to arrange another time with them when the process can be continued.

Now, you, that is to say the Third I you, like a good couples counselor, can sit back in your chair and review what happened with your clients. What were the themes, the predominant emotional trends? What did you feel was the most charged subject? Where did you see the most conflict, the most understanding? Did you feel genuine affection between them, or were they consistently hostile? Did they only speak to you, or did they engage each other in a true dialogue? If they did not manage to communicate with each other, how can you support that next time? If you feel so disposed, make a few notes in the folder that has their names on it. When you feel that you have digested the session, close the folder and put it away.

Now we will slowly exit the "space" where this dialogue has occurred. On the next exhalation, begin to follow the breath toward the point between the eyebrows. We are reversing the course you followed when you began. With each breath, reach forward a bit more until you are making a complete connection between the deep Ajna (Sixth) Chakra, and its more superficial corresponding kshetra [*], at the surface of your forehead. Once that is established, slowly begin to release the connection with the deep point, allowing the course of the breath to shorten toward the front one, until you are again able to rest at the point between the eyebrows.

Pause there for a few respiratory cycles, and re-connect with the consciousness that goes with this point. Now, slowly begin to follow back down the nasal passages toward the starting point, the point between the nostrils. Extend the breath a little further with each exhalation, until you are spanning the whole distance between these two points again. Once more, after you do this, shorten your breath, until you have returned to the point between the two nostrils. Again, rest here for a moment, noticing whether the breath is flowing equally through the left and right. If not, who is predominant, He (right side) or She (left)? Does that jibe with what was happening during the conversation?

Now we will end the meditation by following the breath down through the naso-pharynx and the throat into the chest, again extending your reach a little further with each breath. Once you have reached the center of the chest, the heart, let your attention rest there.

Remember that the heart is the main Wedding Chapel for the inner marriage. Feel the right heart and the left, the receptive, yin aspect of each, and the active yang aspect of each side. Allow yourself to feel the increment of opening your heart has experienced as a result of, at the very least, this sincere attempt to increase the communication and harmony between Him and Her. Let that increase and radiate from the heart, and the love and compassion that it brings shine forth from your fourth (heart) chakra.

Now extend that energy down your arms, right and left. Now extend it upwards to your head, and down to your feet. Remember that the cross is one of the universal symbols for the heart, and notice its centrality in the flow from above down, and below up, and from right to left and left to right. Consider grounding yourself in this heart energy, this outreaching and in moving connectivity between yourself and others that can mirror your own inner relationship that you have just examined, and that can serve to further your capacity to bring it to joyful union.

[*] Each of the (at least 2nd through 6th) chakras has its primary location at or near the spinal column (or, in the case of the 6th, in the center of the skull). There is for each also a corresponding subsidiary representation on the surface of the body.

Now, slowly and gently allow your fingers to move slightly, extending the heart energy out to your hands, which reach into the world and toward other people. Slowly begin to move your head a bit, allowing some of the heart energy to reach there and infuse your thoughts with love and compassion and support the light of Shiva that moves from above through you. Lastly, begin to move your toes again, slowly unfolding your legs with your hands, and massaging them to bring the flow from the heart down to your feet where it can reach into the earth and ground you in Her nurturance and receive Her Life force and Her Power, which is yours.

When salt dissolves,
It becomes one with the ocean,
When my ego dissolved,
I became one with Shiva and Shakti

— Jnaneshvar

PART 2

TANTRA APPLIED

A Commentary on the Dialogue

PART 2

Introduction

I t is customary in the traditions of Tantra to offer a commentary when presenting a dialogue between Shiva and Shakti. The purpose of the commentary is to help the reader understand and apply the insights the dialogue conveys. It is, of course, only one interpretation, and the reader has the freedom (and responsibility) to develop her/his own.

In this commentary, I will suggest that the dialogue, and the Tantra tradition it is based on, are relevant – and even, perhaps, indispensable for the current era. They offer two major perspectives that are largely absent from the Euro-American dominant conversation of the moment: One is on the distinction between Power and Violence; the other is on the role of Pleasure and Play in spirituality.

The first of these involves a totally and radically different concept of *power*. In the tantric worldview power is an attribute of the Feminine. Not of just any aspect of the Feminine, but of the *Yang* Feminine – that is to say Shakti/Kali. In the view of Tantra this is power, and, in fact, the *only* power there is. Other phenomena that we might be inclined to term "power" are not. They must be re-examined and re-named appropriately. Most obviously, much of what we call "power" is abusive and damaging. Tantra would term such "power," *violence.* What is termed *power* in Tantra never has such qualities. It is creative and the essence of life.

This may at first seem like semantic quibbling, but I can assure you that it is not. It is a crucial issue on the planet at this moment, and it is of utmost importance that we acknowledge the distinction between the two: power and violence. As we will see in the following pages, this is not as easy as it might at first seem. Our culture and our institutions are so shot through with violence, and our denial of it is so consistent and determined, that the disentangling of it from true power is a formidable challenge.

But meeting this challenge, difficult though it be, opens the door to a very different way of living on Planet Earth. Pre-eminently it opens the possibility of hanging our spirituality on principles of play, pleasure, and joy – something that represents a decided departure from our approach of recent millennia.

Indeed the vision of spirituality as synchrony with a cosmic dance, a playful exploration of the experiences of life, while it is consonant with what is often called (pejoratively) "new age thought," is at extreme variance with the main-stream of Judeo-Christian traditions of the last several thousand years. Again, this may at first seem like a technical adjustment, but its implications are far-reaching. Try this. Imagine a sermon from a Catholic pulpit lauding an approach to sex as play: "Sexuality is part of the dance of the cosmos – designed by the Divine to delight and instruct."

Again, reframing spirituality as "play" has far-reaching ramifications, and can re-shape much of the social milieu in which we presently exist. Problem is, such a revision hangs on the prior one: the acknowledgement of the pervasiveness of violence and the cessation of its support and perpetuation.

An analysis of violence along tantric lines is the backbone of this second part of the present book. As we move from chapter to chapter, we will layer on bit by bit the different explanations that reveal how violence works, how the trauma it engenders operates to restrict our lives and disempower us, and what we can do to step free of this trap.

In **CHAPTER 1** we start with the Body. Your body is your piece of Gaia. We shall see how the way you relate to it is (very) often a replica of domestic violence. Turned on its head, that fact will offer an amazing opportunity to work out and outgrow some of the culturally implanted violence we all carry. The trick here is it's a bootstrap operation: your body is also your (tantric) instrument of experimentation and life-giving pleasure. And when it's not functioning well, your capacity for the work/play of tantra is grossly inhibited.

In **CHAPTER 2** we turn to Relationships. Relationship spans all the experiences of life. From inner relationships – those that exist between the parts of our selves [*] – and those external connections with others that mirror and are mirrored by the inner ones. We will look at the core dynamics, which run the gamut from fifties sitcom Father Knows Best / Leave it to Beaver, to the ultimate souring of that happy pretense: domestic violence. These prototypical interactions are our common foundation and can help us peg the tendencies and default impulses that keep us confined in the reflex world of frustration and violence.

While those first two chapters constitute a survey of "life without Shakti," or the effort to design a way of living that will eliminate the unpredictable and arational whimsy of the creative life force (the Feminine in various guises – including her more radically transformative aspect, Kali), the remaining chapters focus on our strategies for engaging Her – in one way or another:

CHAPTER 3 is about our relationship with the Environment, which again is a reflexive re-enactment of the domestic violence core dynamic. Bringing this into awareness makes it possible to step around these old (and increasingly dangerous) knee-jerk responses, and craft a new relationship with Nature, one that is full of abundance, excitement, and delight. This, we hope, will replace our current game, which might be termed "Egging Kali On" (at least we get some attention from Her...though it won't be pretty).

CHAPTER 4 turns to our Social/Political/Economic dilemmas. Not surprisingly (by this point) we find that the core dynamic between Masculine and Feminine is again re-enacted. The political/economic elite exploits the lumpen proletariat (human masses) in much the same way as the drunken husband

---

[*] Though beyond the scope of the present book, Tantra both recognizes and addresses the fragmentations of the self – not, however, with the techniques of western psychotherapy and psychoanalysis. It takes what, from the perspective of these western approaches, look like shortcuts: stepping up and back into "meta" levels of awareness to facilitate the integration. e.g., moving to the Heart Chakra through use of mantra or breath or concentration on that chakra to integrate split off sexuality or aggression; or moving up to the Sixth Chakra to integrate Masculine and Feminine.

terrorizes wife and children. (Both might be thought of as aiming to keep Kali from emerging – all the while building to Her wrathful entry.) While the parallels may be more informative than entertaining, the possibilities for a new arrangement are heartening and tantalizing.

Chapter 5 returns to the question of Spirituality. What would a post-violence spirituality look like? If we were to remove the need for (or pretense of) social control in religion, and drop all vestiges of moralism from our collective spiritual life, what delights, potentialities, and fulfillments might await us? Without violence to sabotage the inner marriage, and with the way cleared to move into the union of the inner Masculine and Feminine and fully open the Ajna Chakra, what fun might it be to play on the frontiers beyond time, space, and causality?

And of course, what is necessary to clear the deck for this new world to materialize? This might be termed, "Longing for Kali." We do long for Her to step in and wipe away the structures of the past that confine us, even if we are terrified that She might. In fact, all of these ways of relating to Her: denying Her existence, egging Her on, fearing Her appearance, and longing for Her to rescue us are churning together in our collective psyche. What will emerge? It's going to be a rollercoaster ride, a fun house, and the jackpot at the sharp shooting booth, all rolled into one. Hang onto your guidebook (it's in your hands right now), and let's go!

CHAPTER I

Health and the Body

The inner relationship somatized
~ or Kali denied, part I – She burns the house down ~

The dialogue between Shiva and Shakti both explains and exemplifies the dynamic between them. This creates a context for a re-examination of the multiple crises we find ourselves in at this moment on Planet Earth. Let us begin this commentary cum application of the dialogue by looking at how the core dynamic between Him and Her plays out on the level of our health – of our bodies and how we relate to them.

For many years I practiced holistic medicine, struggling to integrate the approaches of natural medicine within the framework provided by tantra [*]. So allow me to begin this discussion with a case:

David said he was burnt out. He worked eighty hours a week. Though he worked as a healer, he looked not unlike the average 50-year-old man – red-faced, potbellied – angry enough to stay just this side of depression. A psychic had told him that if he continued the way he was going, in a few years he would have "the opportunity to pass over." That got his attention, and he decided that he'd rather make some sort of adjustments so he could stay on the

[*] See *Radical Healing* by the present author which will detail many of the practices and approaches to natural medicine that are in keeping with the philosophy of Tantra as presented in the present work.

planet. He still had work he wanted to do.

As I worked with him, homeopathic remedies emerged as good bets and patterns of relating took shape. He had left his wife because she was, he said, crazy. But from our tantric perspective he was clearly identified with an inner Masculine that was not merely sometimes in gentle disagreement with its Feminine counterpart, as our Shiva and Shakti have modeled, but who was at war with Her. She was, he seemed to feel, unreliable, not nurturing, and liable to irrational fits of pique. He wanted no part of Her.

Embodiment is the sphere of the feminine. She revels in the carnal connection with life on earth, and happily preoccupies herself with its minutiae. In fact, it is often convenient to think of our bodies as our own personal, standard issue piece of Gaia. It is our own little portable experiment in being living matter. But being in a body can be "inconvenient." It's a messy business: Smelly fluids and constant neediness – food, water, rest, and most humiliating of all, touch from others. She (the Feminine in each of us, be we male, female, or some other variant of gender) demands all this incessantly, and seems resistant to reason. She refuses to be put off (at least not for long), and is openly scornful of His (our Masculine's) logic and businesslike agenda.

David wrote Her off. She was impossible. "She is", he confided, "seriously – insane!" Though this was said in reference to his ex-wife, it soon became clear that it applied to most women he knew. And it was, I surmised, how he saw his own Feminine – which he didn't own, but projected on whichever female came near him.

Though David's mother had, according to his account, been unusually distant and his birth especially difficult, he is, as far as I can tell, only a slight exaggeration of what can be seen in many of us – women as well as men. Inside each of us the relationship between inner Masculine and Feminine may be tense and troubled. Though Shakti and Shiva in our dialogue of Part I are cognizant of certain distortions of the masculine and feminine archetypes they exemplify, and are working to shed those (and to inspire us to do likewise), the twisted and tortured versions of Masculine and Feminine that most of us have taken on from our society are far worse.

That is not to say that such acculturation is surprising. In order to accommodate the institutions and pressures of the world we live in, most of us, women and men, identify predominantly with the sort of workaholic Masculine that ruled David. And, like David, this leads us to neglect our bodies. We treat them as irrational pests that are best ignored. What follows, of course is a multiplicity of diseases, the details of which we obsess over – while we don't notice the underlying dynamic responsible: our fundamental estrangement from embodiment.

Medicine, meanwhile, stays busy chasing its tail: contriving endless treatments (many of them toxic and destructive) to block the deterioration of the body, without addressing the root causes. Our attitude toward our bodies and that of the medical establishment which provides a context for our struggle, add up to a potent "catch 22". The only viable way out of the dilemma is to become aware of what we are doing and to address the inner dynamic ourselves. Yet the alertness and insight necessary to do that is blurred and obfuscated by the compromise of our bodily functions – most notably the nervous system. Being befuddled and baffled, we are like the proverbial chicken which can't find its way around a wall (the wall being our compromised health).

Though Tantra is a path of radical experimentation and liberating knowledge of the self, it is, as we have seen, an embodied path. And the instrument of our journey along this path is the body. If it is not clear, vital, and incisive, we will falter as tantrikas—hence the critical role of working with health. Without that any spiritual path (especially Tantra) will be, to a great extent, blocked.

Lewis was a case in point. He had no time for pampering his body. He ate whatever was at hand and sat most of the time at this desk, where books and papers were piled precariously all around. Though he was an advanced and dedicated student of tantric Buddhism, his progress was limited by the break-downs in his body. While his Lama exemplified radiant health, Lewis tried to emulate him through rigid schedules and long hours of poring over his books. Instead of radiant health, the result was tachycardia, atrial fibrillation, asthma, hypertension, sleep apnea, esophageal reflux, Hashimoto's disease, and a score of allergies. He was on an even dozen strong pharmaceutical medications, not to mention lists of herbs and supplements. Most of his symptoms were worse on the left side of his body. "Why does my left side suffer?" he asked. When I explained that the left side is the Feminine, and that he was neglecting Her, he smiled. When that began to make sense to him, I encouraged him to take time, relax, be with his body and ask it – ask Her – what She wanted, then give Her, his feminine, in this case Her physical, corporeal aspect, what she needed. It was important to work with his body, with Her. It – She – needed to feel his concern and attentiveness. "She's going to be hard to convince, She's been put off so much in the past," I warned him.

"And note: you've still expected Her to be there to pump your blood, feed your brain, and draw your breath. You may not have had time for Her, but She had better be on the job, keeping the house, when you decided to show up."

At our next session, Lewis was beginning to see how his relationship to his body was like that of an absent, workaholic husband. "The unnoticed Feminine is really pissed," he remarked. To tell the truth, She was in a rage, he realized, having reached the point of beginning to "wreck the house!" Suddenly his physical collapse was making sense to him.

Of course, Lewis is not unique. Nor is this problem limited to men. Women suffer similarly, if not as severely generally speaking. Their Masculine reflects the same planetary pattern [*]. And this disconnect from the body reverberates holographically throughout life on the planet – showing up, for example, in distorted masculine political and economic forces of competition and exploitation that similarly ignore, neglect and abuse the body of Gaia.

But in this holographic complex, issues with the body and physical health hold a unique place. We are talking about the survival of the individual when we begin to consider the diseases that can supervene and threaten life itself. This is the rich and fetid territory of the Root Chakra – where the fear of annihilation dwells. It has always intrigued me that the cultures of the East, by and large, take more common sense care of their bodies, and despite what often amounts to food shortages and inadequate public hygiene, remain surprisingly healthy – and this in the context of a cosmology that views the body as a mere temporary vehicle, to be cast off when worn out.

Meanwhile, in the West, the body is overstuffed, over drugged, and over stressed, despite the fact that many in this part of the world view their bodies as the sum total of their existence, and believe that when it expires, they will cease to be, their consciousness extinguished with their physiological processes. Is this some macabre dance with annihilation? Is it a desperate attempt to assert autonomy by taking charge of ones own destruction?[**]
While the answers to those questions remain a mystery, it seems clear that there is a great struggle going on in the territory of the Root Chakra – an overwhelming preoccupation with a pervasive sense of "the futility of life," and a lack of any felt nurturance from the Cosmic Feminine. He in his arrogant exploitation of Her, projects his own contempt and indifference and thus assumes She feels that for him. He fears She will turn on him, and when

---

[*] Note that when we move to speaking of women, we talk about "their Masculine," relating to their Feminine, whereas Lewis spoke of himself relating to Her. Herein lies an advantage that women have currently. Generally, they more easily step back from their Masculine and can observe it. Men identify with it tenaciously. Ultimately Lewis's path to health will necessitate that he come to observe not just Her, but Her and Him.

[**] Classics of our literature, such as Poe's "*The Masque of the Red Death*" hint that this may be true.

She does – in the guise of Kali – to "burn down the house" and set him free from his stalemate, he only sees retribution and viciousness, rather than the liberation She brings.

Preoccupation with fear – actually *terror* is a more accurate term – and the desperately denied conviction that he is ultimately to be annihilated prevent him from being open to Her playful spontaneous creations, and the limitless love and nurturance She offers. Of course, he is ultimately to be annihilated – at least that current ego, constructed as it is around the denial that he has a Feminine and that She is his power. His recovery involves: first admitting and owning his fear; then entering it and discovering its link with the undesirable ego; and last, joyfully liberating himself from the chains of that now obsolete version of ego.

After this tantric analysis of our relationship to our bodies, let us look at a tantric solution to the disastrous situation with our health that has resulted from it.

The basic challenge is to uncover our own pure Her – the essential, unsullied version of our Feminine—She who nurtures us, and who guides our actions, decisions and way of living. Or, at least, *potentially* guides us. To find that deeper, inherently powerful and loving aspect of ourselves, of the Universe as present within us, we must also uncover our own pure Masculine. That will usually be necessary since most of us are firmly positioned in the Masculine as we relate to our bodies. We have identified with Him and relate to Her through Him. And we have assumed all His violent, abusive attitudes, and his fear and rejection of Her. To be able to even acknowledge that She is there, that we are in part Her, we need to uncover a less distorted Masculine from which to look for Her. In other words, we must find Shiva as well as Shakti within.

And our dialogue presented us with the principles according to which we can accomplish that. To wit:

Remember that everything is an experiment. Therefore approach interactions with our bodies, our dietary choices and our herbal teas or exercise sessions, as experiments. We try what we feel inclined to try, or what captures our curiosity, and then we observe carefully, gathering data. She will never be averse to that, since She loves attention. By following this principle, we become attentive.

Use tapas around what are observed to be damaging habits (*if* they are "ripe for plucking,"—in other words, if we are ready to let them go. There will generally be one, even if it's a small habit, that is ready to be worked with.) Allow tapas to release energy tied up in the targeted habit that can power your body to make new choices, actions, creations, and observe and appreciate what it's doing.

Harness the yang masculine – the phallic – by cultivating and going with your curiosity, your desire to understand, to penetrate into the mystery of why and how your body functions.

Study your outer relationships – with a partner, or a boss, or a friend – to pinpoint the dynamics that you might find in your relationship to your body, and then see if that us what is going on – check it out.

Notice how bringing more of the light of consciousness down into the inner workings of your physical body automatically changes the way it functions. When you actually *locate* your liver, and you can feel the congestion or discomfort after you have that third cup of coffee, does it begin to respond differently to what you put in your stomach? Or does feeling its uneasiness shift the way its dysfunction leads into anger?

How is your body the battleground for your inner gender war? Notice the connections between what is going on between your Masculine and Feminine on the one hand, and the tensions, spasms, blocks, and complaints of your body on the other.

Finally, look for the pleasure. Where and when does it register? Remember that She is a pleasure generator. She is designed to experience pleasure. But she needs Him to create the container, to bring the light of awareness for it to reach the level of delight and joy that is possible. Learn what you can do that gives your body pleasure. Don't be stingy with it. Then work with your body so its capacity to experience pleasure is expanded, extended. By attentive tending of it, you cultivate its sensitivity, rather than blunting it, as is done when you're inattentive, impatient, indifferent to it.

This is what my teacher, Swami Rama, used to call "making obstacles into means." The very impediment to our progress along the tantric path becomes the opportunity to learn Tantra and to develop an embodied appreciation of the verity of its principles.

Using such an approach to our bodies brings us into a Masculine curiosity and insight (the phallic) and patient containment and care (the testicular) that are relatively free of the usual distortions that afflict Him. In other words, we are becoming Shiva. That purer Masculine will be able to see and honor Her, and their loving interaction begins to open the Ajna Chakra (Third Eye/I).

So we see that working with the body is a complete tantric practice in itself! Therefore it is an excellent starting place, since it leads us into an understanding of how to weave together the various principles and their application. Moreover, it clears and refines the very instrument of Tantra, the body itself. Tantra is an embodied spirituality. The body must be capable of holding the energy implied by that. Getting it in order clears the way for new explorations and discoveries.

And last but not least, the body is a microcosm of the larger world, where we will use the same principles and meet analogous challenges. Working with it hones the skills we will need to practice Tantra in the other domains of life. [*] The first of these is the realm of relationship.

---

[*]   This treatment of Health and the Body my feel insufficient to many. No doubt it is, but more detail can be found in an earlier book I did titled *Radical Healing*. While it seldom explicitly mentions Tantra, it is consistently shaped around the Tantra principles offered in this present book, and can be profitably read as an extension of this chapter.

CHAPTER 2

Relationship and the Core Dynamic

The inner relation acted out

~ or Kali denied, part II: trying to make a life without Her ~

As we learned in our dialogue, She resides "in" the left side of the body (and therefore the right brain, we like to say today). Those territories are activated when I breathe through my left nostril. This is not merely a quaint folk belief. Research confirms it. More importantly, however, it is a palpable, verifiable experience. If I pay close attention, I will discover that I am a different person when my breath flows primarily through the left nostril than I am when it flows through the right. She comes to life when I breathe through the left side, He when it's the right.

Unfortunately, we don't often take note of this difference, nor the shift from one to the other (nostril flow switches sides every couple of hours). Our lack of awareness of something so immediate and important is an indication of the degree to which these two aspects of ourselves are not integrated, but function in a sort of schizoid, disconnected fashion.

They need not remain so. This dynamic is a central linchpin in personal and planetary transformation, and bringing it into awareness is of utmost importance. There are clues to how to do this in the traditional teachings of tantric yoga. They focus awareness on this alternating breath, and invite us to look for the point of integration (where both nostrils flow equally). This latter is termed *sushumna* for those who have made it to intermediate yoga. The confluence of the left and right enable the opening of the Third Eye (sixth chakra). The consciousness that then emerges brings a unified perspective – to replace the two separate ones with their continual shifting back and forth.

However, this is not a realm where our mechanistic laws of cause and effect operate neatly. So it's not quite so simple as "making the breath equal in order to open the Sixth Chakra." That's only more mechanistic arrogance. A more gentle, less forced approach is needed. Recall the "marriage counseling" approach we took in the He/She meditation. This actually sets the Sixth Chakra into motion – activation – by having it serve the function that it is designed for.

But while the meditation – the He/She inner dialogue—is of inestimable value, don't expect it to be all sweetness and light – or even as light-heartedly contentious as that we saw between Shiva and Shakti in our text. If you are typical, your Feminine has likely been ignored a long time and might well not be very happy about that.

In one of my workshops, I led an experiential wedding ceremony between the internal Masculine and Feminine. A participant came up to me at the break, looking upset. I asked what was wrong. "In a nutshell," he blurted, "She said to me, 'you're talking about marriage and we're not even engaged!!'" I laughed and suggested we have lunch together to discuss the situation. But by midday, he felt less panicky. "I talked with Katy" (one of the staff members), he explained, "and she said, 'Just send Her flowers.'" "Perfect," I agreed.

It was, in fact, a great first step. The Feminine in most of us (men and women) has been taken for granted and abused for so many years that a little (or even a lot) of remedial attention is in order. But my workshop participant was still not fully into the process. It was he, himself, who was talking to Her. In other words, he was identifying with his Masculine, rather than with the Third Eye consciousness. When you do this inner work, it's important that you not identify with either your Masculine or your Feminine. Because most of us are so tightly gender bound, that's easier said than done. At least it was for me. I had to be jostled loose by Her.

I was a participant in a workshop in the hills of Northern California. My small group decided to do a full moon ritual. We invented this as we went – all of the six men were spiritual teachers of some sort. Though we allowed time for each of us to address the moon in our own individual ways during the experience, the common theme was an honoring of the Goddess, and an invitation for

Her to be more present in our lives. I was unaware of the power of such a rite until I sat the next day in an open meadow on a hillside nearby for a private meditation. A feminine "voice" – one with impressive presence and considerable *shakti* showed up forcefully in my inner space.

At first I was delighted. We began to "talk."[*] But the inner conversation was suddenly interrupted when She asked, "Why do you keep addressing me as 'you?'"

"Why wouldn't I?" I asked, surprised.

"Because I *am* you," She replied.

"Now wait a minute!" I shot back, feeling this was getting uncomfortably out of hand. "I acknowledge you are a part of my inner world, but you are *you*, and I am *me!*"

"Wrong," She corrected me calmly and clearly. "*I am you.*"

Her voice carried an authority and clarity that mine lacked. I gradually accepted that She was indeed me. But it was awhile before I realized that "He" was also me – in the same way. Then I was able to put Her and Him on an equal footing as two fundamental components of myself. And that perspective was only possible from a higher vantage point – that of the "Third I"/Third Eye, the sixth chakra. This is a new sense of self, one that does not identify with either our masculine or feminine selves.

This inner relationship between Feminine and Masculine is the core dynamic, the whirling of electron around proton, the fundamental building block of the universe. It is always and forever a dance of opposites, a tension and an attraction, that keeps the process moving and life continuing.

But the dynamic, like the masculine and feminine archetypes that are the heart of it, are subject to distortions that they take on as the result of the cumulative habits of interaction that are dominant in families, in cultures, and on the planet as a whole. And currently, those distortions are especially

[*] Though I present the following as a dialogue, the same caveats offered with the He/She meditation are applicable here: The "voice" of the Feminine may be – and for me was – not so much a voice heard as a largely non-verbal communication with Her presence. Since that is very difficult to convey, I am making all the communications verbal.

In any event, the degree to which the Feminine (or the Masculine) is experienced as separate from you, will vary from person to person – especially at the beginning of this inner exploration. As we see a bit further along in this anecdote, men will tend to view their Feminine as "other," while women tend to view their Masculine as "other." As identification shifts from ones anatomical sex – or gender identity—to the "Third I/Eye," however, one begins to see both Masculine and Feminine as "other" than this more integrated new identity. This new sense of self is the identity of the Inner Marriage, the Integral, the consciousness of the Sixth Chakra, beginning to dawn.

dramatic. The result is that the Masculine and Feminine and their interaction, within us as well as out in the world around us, serve as shapers of institutions. They are determiners of how we behave toward the earth and toward those peoples who are of color, or indigenous – who are of the earth. All these, and many other of our relational experiences, are affected by that primal Masculine/Feminine dynamic and as a result, manifest a deep and abiding conflict, a sort of gender war that cuts through every level of our existence.

This war, whether the battle ground be the family dynamic, environmental issues, the political and economic dominance of the haves over the have nots, or simply the inner spaces of our own psyches, shows many of the same characteristics: She has been exploited, He is cut off from Her, and thus deprived of his access to power. So He resorts to brutal control and abuse out of frustration and impotence. Our cultures strain to deny the fact that power is of the Feminine, to kow-tow to the patriarchal rulers in order to preserve our social standing and our livelihoods, while that system preys on the desperate consumerism that runs rampant in populations that are bereft of the joy that comes from spontaneity and creative self-expression (spanda).

This twisted, violent dynamic, so pervasive in the outside world, fuels such tragedies as child abuse. To those stifled and constrained by the fear of spontaneity and battling the emergence of the Feminine which brings it, the effervescence of childhood is a constant affront – annoying, irritating, and eventually even infuriating. Such patterns gradually shape character to accommodate them, thus moving inside – to the inner, the infrastructure, of the psyche. And then, as we act from that foundation, the inner distorted Masculine and Feminine, in turn, begin to build, and eventually sustain, a world that reflects their war. It might be helpful to identify the typical—or rather prototypical—dynamic characteristic of this "perpetual war." To chose a prototype, we would do well to look at a couple deadlocked in domestic violence:

She (let's call her Mary) is exhausted, angry, unsatisfied – sexually and otherwise—and desperate. He (John) is baffled, depressed, cut off from any sense of authentic spontaneity or creative power, frustrated, irritated and given to outbursts of impotent rage. Mary has tried everything to break the deadlock, hoping to jar him loose from his rigidity. She has tried making their surroundings more attractive, and herself as well. She has met his indifference with cheerful smiles and encouragement.

When that failed, she tried being more assertive, presenting logical arguments for why they need to work together to make an enjoyable life. Finally she has withdrawn from him to some extent, saving her energy for work and the kids.

John finds Mary to be annoying, nagging, chronically needy. He sees her as emotionally disturbed. She is, though in a different sense of the expression from what he means: She is disappointed, feels the energy of her body thwarted in its need to experience touch, tenderness and pleasure. The chronic blockage of the flow of life – of a fullness of living leaves her feeling restless, at odds with her nature.

John sees her as irrational. And she is sometimes, but is more often *arational*, sensing the emptiness of rational discussions of matters of heart, body and soul. He concludes that she's just a whiney mess. It is clear to him why women are considered inferior to men: it's because they *are*.

What is especially infuriating to John, though he would be unlikely to be able to articulate this, is how often Mary refuses to sink into the kind of negativity that he is immersed in. Despite his verbal and sometimes physical abuse, she doggedly remains committed to her home, her children, and sometimes even to some shred of meaningfulness she can find in the work she does outside the home. Though she often feels hopeless and sometimes loses herself in nervous overeating or crying spells, she keeps coming round for another stab at one more way to make things work, even to just survive, and still have a bit of life as a family.

In other words, Mary continues to reveal her creativity, her shakti, her power to manifest life, even when it is grossly attenuated by exhaustion and despair. She has that power, that deeply rooted drive to give life and to birth. She really can't hide it, even though she knows his seeing it might throw him into another dangerous rage. She uses her power, and her nurturance, for those she loves, because she can't do otherwise. It's who she is.

And yes, this is a grating affront to John. How dare she? How dare she have the power that is rightfully his? He is supposed to be the strong one – the one who can come up with a solution, save the day. He is sure she is ridiculing him (and this is the thing he can least tolerate.) Eventually all she has to do is walk in the room and he is enraged. Finally he gives in and hits her. Then, because that releases some of his pent up rage, he hits her again.

As horrifying as this is, it is not rare. Though the details of the dynamic vary, this scene is repeated in many places every day. It is the shadow dynamic of our relationships – not just outer, but often between our own Masculine and Feminine within. Certainly between our minds and our bodies, as we saw in the last chapter. Clearly between our environment and us, as we shall see in the next chapter. And even between our patriarchal systems of government, finance, and corporate control and the people they dominate. How did this come to be?

While much of the evolution of this disturbed dynamic will have to be left to the future historians, who will have more of the requisite distance on their subject than we do at present, bits and pieces of the story have already been gathered by writers and researchers. Assembling them into a coherent picture may still be premature, but I will venture a preliminary sketch.

History Of A Marriage On The Rocks

Certainly the rise of the prestige of the intellectual at the time of the Renaissance and the Enlightenment, was part and parcel of the discrediting of the Feminine, and contributed mightily to the elevation of rationality and linear thinking to the acme of social influence. While the status of women was equal to –or in some cases greater than—that of men in many indigenous cultures, those countries who considered themselves "civilized" tended to bend to the winds of the times and enthrone the left brain, linear thinking, and the goals of material acquisition and economic "growth," elevating them to a position of near Divinity. As the Natural world became merely a conglomeration of resources to be exploited, women, whose nature is strongly allied to that of Gaia, became similarly regarded: their nurturance and their caring for home and family could be taken for granted and even tapped for use when they were put into positions of support in the office, or the hospital or the factory.

As long as a woman's role is confined to the Yin Feminine, she is exploitable. She will keep trying to nurture life – no matter what, because she *cares*. If she can be induced to stay in this yin space, and prevented from shifting into the Yang Feminine—her Kali mode—she can be relied on to keep on giving and giving and giving to the point of depletion and collapse.

As their status dropped, women increasingly became seen as inferior. While the framers of the American constitution at the turn of the nineteenth century emulated certain of the features of the agreements of the Iroquois Confederation, they neglected to give women the vote. The Iroquois, by contrast, allowed only men to hold office, but only *women* could vote.

Meanwhile, the ascendancy of the rational favored ever more analysis, breaking everything down into fragments in order to understand and deal with it. This was not merely a mode of operation, it was a mode of perception, a characteristic of the Structure of Consciousness itself. Once it became thoroughly engrained in the infrastructure of the mind, it was invisible and escaped notice.

But its impact was dramatic. Now gender was split in a much more drastic way than before. Though the roles of Masculine and Feminine had been rather strictly allotted according to anatomical sex in earlier ages, the difference then was one of polarity: i.e., I would have experienced my maleness/masculinity as one end of a pole, with your femaleness/femininity at the other. Though we were opposite extremes in this respect, we were still connected – united, in fact – by the pole itself. This is the nature of gender in the mythical consciousness – the sort of relationship that we saw between Shiva and Shakti in the dialogue of Part I, and that we find in our own inner version of that.

This is experientially quite a different perception from that of a duality: with duality the connection is severed. We are two distinct and essentially different entities. There is no inner connection that allows me to resonate with your way of being. We have been split asunder, never to be reunited. Though I, as a man, may be joined to you, a woman, in marriage, we will be two totally different beings with no inner frame of reference to clue us into what the other is about. Of course we did not cease to have an inner contrasexual – every man still had a Feminine and a Masculine, as did every woman – but the temper of the time demanded that it not be seen or acknowledged (even to oneself).

This rupture led to a strong sense of separateness and an ego structure (especially among men – who were exclusively identified with the new dry, sterile, linear/rational thought) that saw worth measured in contrast to someone else's. In this way a man's self respect came to be hinged hugely on not resembling a woman – his self worth could collapse in a flash if he were even suspected of being—in any way—feminine. In fact, he could not be *feminine*; if he showed such traits, he was termed "effeminate" – or "effete," or any number of other such pejorative adjectives.

He was trained from birth to eschew all things that would make him look like a girl. When the Spanish came to the New World and found the *berdaches* – the "two spirited" natives who were aware of both their masculine and feminine natures (the males of which would dress freely as women, and gladly have sex with other men) – they were so horrified and disgusted they had them fed live to the dogs. Their justification for such atrocities was that the berdaches "*debase* themselves to be as women," so clearly had to be annihilated. The Feminine of the patriarchal male had been utterly banished from his inner world. Or, at least, he was not, under any circumstance, to acknowledge – or even be conscious of – Her presence.

This would not have been so disastrous, were it not for the fact that She, his inner Feminine, included his *shakti*, his power. Without that, he was severely crippled. But he was the cripple who must hide his infirmity. He was in a position of authority. He could not be weak, powerless. So he had to – has had to right up to the present time – keep up the pretense of power. How can one hide so grievous a deficiency? It must be done like the magician: by distraction. So if I cannot demonstrate authentic power – an ability to create, to give birth to something truly new and valuable – then I must, as Shiva explained to Shakti in our dialogue, "shock and awe" you. This I do with brute (and often brutal) acts of violence. I crush the opposition. I sentence many to death. I send out the military to annihilate my enemies. So there, doesn't that prove that I'm powerful? Well, no, as a matter of fact, it doesn't.

Power is not the ability to destroy. It is the ability to create, to manifest, to birth. No amount of shock and awe should distract us from that truth. But it has. Centuries of patriarchal rule, its control of the channels of communication, and its ability to intimidate and threaten, have allowed it to sell its violence as power. The meaning of the words has been altered. Everyone now speaks of those who use brute force to intimidate, control, and to quash the creativity of others as "powerful." We say they "walk the halls of power." In an article in the New Yorker in April 2008, a political writer is quoted as saying, "Power is the ability to get others to do what you want and prevent them from doing what you don't want." Most folks would nod and agree.

But this definition of power is 180 degrees off from that implicit in the teachings of Tantra, as expounded by Shiva, and modeled by Shakti. According to those teachings, power is the personal, spanda-based expression of ones own creative energy. Conventional thinking might object that getting others to do what you envision is what creativity is all about; that this is how the personal vision is made manifest. But there is no room in the tantric concept of power for such an appropriation of the energy of others. That would amount to enslavement. While leadership might be seen as inspiring others to realize their own capacity for self-expression, manipulating them to express your vision is very "old paradigm" and at the root of patriarchal exploitation.

Men aren't supposed to have feelings or needs, notes Marshall Rosenberg, creator of Non Violent Communication training. They do as they are told—by an officer or a superior. This is a potential set up for violence: They are not to listen to the signals that would allow them to respond to spanda.

As for the male, it only remains to repeat what Shiva so vividly described: bereft of his power, he is a fake. Unfortunately this persona of the male is what we incorporate as our inner Masculine. We take it in from our fathers, from the characters in the movies we watch, from the guy across the street whom we idolize because he's cool and he talks with us. Thus the metamorphosis of the Masculine has occurred gradually over the centuries, leaving our psyche with a twisted and deformed masculine archetype.

The story of the evolution of the Feminine is the counterpart to this. The Euro-centric cultures gradually divested the Feminine of the aura of power. This process has been detailed elsewhere [*] and it is generally accepted that it was accelerated during the Inquisition, when women who were determined to own their Yang Feminine, their power, were systematically singled out and exterminated. It is estimated that the women thus executed during the infamous "witch hunts" of the era numbered in the millions.

Once the Yang Feminine was banished from the culture, its institutions, its art, its iconography, women were left with no cultural archetype for their power. It was as though it had never existed. The very means of communication and even thought – the language – had been virtually purged of evidence of spanda, of play and pleasure as essential aspects of what gives life meaning and substance. Women were caught in an impossible bind. They, as the cultural custodians of the Feminine, were forbidden even to *know* that it was the power that created and sustained everything around them. They may have known – and surely often did know – in their bones that this was true, but the words to express it, the cultural symbols and role models, the stories and traditions, were eerily absent.

Meanwhile, they had to cope with the issue of survival – survival in a world of violence, where survival was tenuous – certainly survival of the body, but more so, of the soul. And their very being was overwhelmed by the effort to provide protection for their children, their families, and somehow to still ensure the joy without which life is not possible. To do the impossible, they split off part of their psyche and sold it to the devil: it would pick up the weapon of the men, it would traffic in violence, it would fight brutality with brutality – emotionally, if possible, viciously if necessary, even physically if pushed to the wall. This became the compromise that would allow the woman/wife/mother to protect life. Yet at the same time, she had to preserve a space within herself and within her home for the safety, the protection, the freedom from survival issues that would allow the playful and pleasurable unfoldment of vibrant living souls.

[*] For example, see the work of Rianne Eisler, especially her well known book, *The Chalice and the Blade*, which offers an intriguing (if contested) account of this process.

She accomplished this in varying ways. Sometimes it was by condoning and even supporting the violence on the part of her spouse who would agree to keep it confined to the outside world, and by colluding in the pretense that it didn't exist (the Mafia wife) – to live, in other words, a sort of schizophrenia, maintaining a faux paradise within the walls of the home, but leaving reality a dark secret that her children might stumble upon at adolescence.

Sometimes it was by moving the schizophrenic split inside herself – wielding guilt and shame to squelch the spanda of her children so they could survive, when she knew that to express it would make them too vulnerable to the world of violence that they were immersed in. This of course contradicted the very safety and protection that she was struggling to provide, and she struggled with the unreality that the double messages created and that threatened frequently to engulf her.

Sometimes she remained a calm, loving, presence, and denied the violence that drove the world outside, and that seeped into her home and life at every turn, and made living a constant pushing away of reality.

And there are many other arrangements she made. In each case, it was a balancing act, the accomplishment of the impossible. But it generally allowed her some sort of access to the pseudo power that was wielded by the male of the patriarchal world – either in a modulated form through him, or from herself and her access to her own (distorted) Masculine.

For it was not so forbidden for a woman to act from her Masculine as it was for a man to act from his Feminine. In fact, it was at times rewarded. It was, after all, a step up in prestige – to the vaunted superiority of the man. There was only one condition: she had to do so as a woman acting in the manner of a man. The one thing that was forbidden (and feared) was for her to act from her *Yang* Feminine. That was dreaded and verboten.

So women led the way in acknowledging the dual aspect of the inner world. They owned their Masculine – even their Phallic capacity – and created a revolution that over centuries gained momentum and came to be called feminism. It's acceptance was a compromise. Better let them into the men's club, than drive them to discover the Kali within.

So she had to surrender her power at the door. What's more, the Masculine that she could access was that of an archetype that was rotten – twisted with rage, collapsed with impotence within and inflated with sadism and arrogant violence without. To wield that was both her last resort and a betrayal of her essential nature. It was a "Sofie's choice" [*] too gruesome to contemplate.

Tantra as Alchemy

As we look at this narrative, this long road descending into a relational hell, it is heartening to note that much of this most likely would not have happened, had men and women been fully aware that they were each really both Feminine and Masculine, that they had this dual nature that offers – even demands – that both be employed, that they both be given voice, that life is a dance of both Feminine and Masculine, of the left as well as the right side of the body, that She needs his abiding and patient support to do Her amazing birthing, that His light of consciousness is indispensable to illuminate the dark recesses of the animal passions, so that they can be freed to power the brilliance of human creativity and delight.

Well, that's what might have prevented us from getting into this mess. But apparently we weren't ready for that degree of awareness at the time that we sunk into violence and war. And we did muck up our inner gender archetypes. What do we do now to climb out of the miserable hole that we're in?

First and foremost, we must not only (belatedly) own our bisexuality, we must own our quadrisexuality. We must come to see and remember that we are not merely He and She, but we are two He's and two She's: We have a Yang Masculine (phallic) and a Yin (testicular) – all of us do – even those in a female body! And we each have a Yin Feminine (nurturing womb), and, when She is ready – when it strikes her fancy, a Yang Feminine (birthing womb), even those of us with a male body! And we must realize that this is true not only in the microcosm (or inner world), but in the "mesocosm" (our relationships with others and the political/social/economic realm). And that it is also true in the macrocosm: Heaven and Earth, the positive and negative energies of the universe—and probably on levels that we haven't yet discovered exist!

We have to "clean up" our inner and outer representations of these fundamental archetypal forces, by grasping how they function on all levels, by uncovering their essential and enduring qualities, and monitoring how they express through us, dropping the contaminating conditionings that they have accrued, and bringing their pure, pristine versions into play within us, and,

---

[*] The allusion here is to a film portraying the dilemma of a mother in a Nazi camp who was told to chose which of her two children would be killed.

with that foundation, into the world in the form of integrated/Integral Consciousness and action.

Actually, the history of the evolution of our primal relationship dynamic is merely the back story for the transformational work with relationship. For it is the background information and understanding that we need to set up our tantric laboratory. And it will be an *alchemical* laboratory.

The tantrica is fundamentally an alchemist. In fact, in the Indic traditions, alchemy is a sub-discipline of Tantra [*]. Alchemy is the science of transformation. It is especially an exploration of the dynamic interaction between the inner transformation and the outer. The alchemist classically combined within his test tube, or glass retort, two substances, most typically mercury and sulfur. Their interaction was considered the Alchemical Marriage, and both mirrored, and was catalyzed by, the corresponding marriage between the Masculine and Feminine principles within the alchemist.

However, there is an intriguing difference between the Alchemy of Tantra and that of the West. European Alchemy sees mercury as the Feminine –the cool and changeable liquid metal. And sulfur, the hot and reactive, the red and powerful reagent that acts on the mercury is its Masculine. The warrior is He, the subject, the recipient, is She. Indian alchemy turns that arrangement on its head: She is the active one. She is the hot, red, sulfur—burning, acting, transforming. He is the cool Mercury, the silver light, the semen of Shiva.

Taking our cues from the dialogue, we might say that the European version of alchemy focused on the Yin Feminine and the Yang Masculine, while the Indic one focused on the Yang Feminine and the Yin Masculine. In other words, the Indic is focusing on the transformative axis, as Shiva described them, while the European is more interested in the stabilizing or sustaining axis (see Figures 4 and 5, Part I, pages 52 and 59). The Indic choice is in keeping with the intent of Alchemy: to probe the mysteries of transformation. The European version is certainly in keeping with that culture's prevalent characterization of Masculine and Feminine. But that fits poorly with the study of transformation. Were the European alchemists confused? Or were they dissembling, as they are known to have done frequently – hiding the radical truths they espoused to protect themselves from the dominant forces in society who would have seen their true goals as disruptive, even dangerous, a threat to the preservation of the status quo?

[*] See David Gordon White, *The Alchemical Body.*

In any case, an alchemical lab might be the best metaphor for the work the tantrica does. The alchemist was preoccupied with the connection or resonance between the chemical reaction in his test tube, or his retort, and the process of change and transformation within himself. If he could somehow harness his own inner process to that within his glass container, they could act as mutual catalysts for one another.

Exactly how this was accomplished (and even whether it was) has remained a matter of much speculation [*]. In the case of the tantric work it is accomplished by a tandem awareness: awareness of my inner process coupled with awareness of my outer interactions with the world.

For example, I am watching my own inner masculine/feminine dynamic via observations gleaned during meditation and during my reactions to events around me. I notice that when I respond freely and those around me are jarred by my frankness, for example, my inner masculine berates my feminine/spanda, and chides her for not being more cautious and controlled. Though there is a legitimate role here for the yin masculine (testicular/tapas), the unadulterated masculine does not resort to shaming.

At the same time, as I am keeping an eye on this tendency, I observe myself with a partner, who blurts out a reaction to the plate just set down in front of us by an elegant waiter, and I, reflexively, start to scowl and say "Shhh!"

In this example the outer is mirroring the inner. But it's more than a mere reflection. The alchemy of it runs deeper than that. Between the alchemist's chemical reaction in the retort and his own internal process of fusion or fission of parts of the self, there existed a sort of mutual stimulation or catalytic action. In other words, each supported and encouraged the other until there was a building crescendo of action that culminated in the transformation – both the inner one and the outer counterpart. One could not succeed without the other. This dynamic of inner/outer change is the characteristic mark of the alchemical work. [**]

So we would be justified if we termed the relational work that is so central to Tantra *alchemical*. Because of the awkwardness of trying to describe the different inner and outer pairings and their relationship, we can use this term as a sort

[*]   David Gordon White, in his scholarly volume, *The Alchemical Body*, offers some evidence that
       alchemists have, and in recent times, continued to effect the transformations they are famous for,
       including on the level of physical matter.
[**]   Of course, Alchemy is even more complex and rich than this alone would suggest.

of shorthand. [*] This synchronous work, inner and outer, paired in the alchemical fashion, is a major feature of Tantra. In fact, it might be accurate to say that without this dimension, the work is not Tantra. It might be an erotic ritual, but without the intent to promote the inner marriage, it is not authentic Tantra. [**]

It is therefore all but impossible to lead those who have no awareness of their essential bisexuality [***] into the study and practice of Tantra. This is even truer for those who are outright resistant to becoming aware of this dual nature. Another implication of this line of thought is that it makes little difference whether the outer relationship is between two people of opposite sex or two of the same sex – or transgendered, or whatever. For the relationship between Masculine and Feminine outside can be between my Masculine and your Feminine, or my Feminine and your Masculine – regardless of which anatomical sex either of us is. It's really immaterial. Only the body is "material," and it *can* matter in certain ways: in a female, for example, there is more "physiological support" for expressing the Feminine. This includes hormones, genitals, etc. And there is the overwhelming pressure during childrearing and later by peers to identify with the Feminine if you have a female body. The corresponding pressures can be as strong or even stronger if you are male.

Nevertheless, the possibility is there, and in fact, it is hardly rare for even a strongly heterosexual couple to switch roles, back and forth, depending on what is happening, and on what prior relational habit is being reactivated. One sex educator I knew personally confided that in his relationship with his wife, there were moments during intercourse when his experience of the penis connecting them switched back and forth between feeling that he was penetrating her, and feeling as though she were penetrating him.

His level of awareness of such subtleties was, no doubt, higher than that of the average person, if for no other reason, by virtue of his work. More often, such subtle shifts in role happen without either party noticing.

---

[*]   The alchemical relationship has also been used to mean looking at the "space" between two people as the retort. See Nathan Schwartz-Salant.

[**]   By that criterion, many of the modern, especially Western practices that call themselves Tantra would not be.

[***] It should be clear by now that in the context of this discussion the term *bisexuality* indicates the inner Masculine and Feminine, not the question of sexual orientation or choice of sexual partners. Nevertheless, it does imply that we each have a significant potential for sexual connection with those of the same sex – since, e.g., a man's Masculine can obviously engage another man's Feminine. (This does not address the possibility that a man's Masculine can engage another man's Masculine – another and very different phenomenon.) The whole question of what sexuality will look like in its probable diverse forms after the activation of the Third Eye/Third I is rich and complex and must remain the subject for another book.

While consciousness of your use of your Masculine and Feminine may not be the only way toward further integration and unfoldment, it is a key part of the tantric path that we are here describing. Such awareness is part and parcel of the gradual activation and the eventual full awakening of the Ajna Chakra (Third Eye).

Those who are more flexible in their gender identity, who have more conscious experience in flowing from one to the other, are likely to be better equipped to be guides for those who are learning to work toward the inner marriage. Hence, gays, lesbians, bisexuals, and other queer people and gender renegades who may have developed such an integrated awareness are excellent candidates for leadership in the teaching of Tantra.

While many traditions acknowledge the "psychological bisexuality" of the human, probably it is Tantra that remains the most obvious example, with its half and half god/goddess. In western thought the awareness of this dual identity was (re)discovered by Carl Jung, and became a cornerstone of his analytical psychology. One might see him as prescient, since his work was followed by a century of social turmoil in the arena of gender issues: feminism, soaring divorce rates, gay, and eventually transgender, liberation and a concomitant agonizing and still far from completed effort to redefine the parameters of masculinity.

Yet the notion of the inner contrasexual (as Jung called our other side) has not really permeated popular culture. Even popular western versions of Tantra are usually limited to a focus on the interaction with a partner of the opposite sex, rather than the relationship between the masculine and feminine aspects of ones inner psyche. (In fact, Jung didn't really address this head-on either.) The result is an irresistible pressure to project the repressed, disowned, and unconscious contrasexual onto someone "out there," most often someone of the opposite sex. This "projective sexual identity" then sets the stage for a battle between the genders that is waged outside in the external world, rather than internally.

What will a post-opening of the Third Eye relationship look like? We don't know, of course, but it's a good bet that it will no longer be merely the playing out of old troublesome dynamics that are arising to be cast off. Nor will it be the prelude to or the preparation for the inner marriage either, for that will have been consummated. It will have to be, we might conclude, the living-happily-ever-after that follows. And how might that look?

We might guess that its major feature will be relatedness for the sheer joy of it – a dance of some sort. Not a plan to be implemented, but the interplay of the spandas of two whole persons who can present and respond to each other in the fullness of their spontaneity.

If each input from one of the partners is offered without agenda – i.e., with authentic spanda—it will trigger from the other…who knows what? We won't know because it also springs from spanda, and that mutual free authentic expression yields an emerging process that is totally unpredictable. It will be a creation that is not "manufactured" (in the way a planned object would be) but is, rather, a never ending free flowing living stream. Living, because the process of life is the constant birthing of the new. It will, then, be something distinct from and larger than either party. Something that can, in fact, contain and transport them, calling each into on-going surrender and transformation. [*]

---

[*]   In the words of Nana Hendricks and Colby Collins, a young couple teaching Tantra in the U.S., it is "God looking into the eyes of God and being seen by God" – their experience of union with each other after each has (re)established her/his own inner union between the Masculine and Feminine.

CHAPTER 3

The Environment: a Visit to Permaculture

Wherein I, the author, whisk You, the reader,
away for an excursion into
The Marriage Made Tangible.

~ or How to avoid the domestic violence dynamic
—on the environmental level—and quit "egging Kali on." ~

Let's imagine for a moment that you allow me to transport you from your suburban home—or your downtown apartment, or wherever you ordinarily live—to consider a new residence and a new life. We will visit friends of mine who have a little homestead for sale on the outskirts of the suburbs.

I am taking you to see how one can live more in touch with Her – Nature, Gaia. To see how to live your life in a way that fosters a harmonious relationship between Her and Him – the Masculine that humans express as they relate to the Feminine in the form of Nature. The tantric principle here is that a caring, attentive attitude toward Her will resonate with and nudge into reconfiguration our own inner Masculine/Feminine dynamic.

As we get out of the car, I explain: What we are to see is only part structure, it is also a total designed environment – i.e., it includes outdoor "living spaces," as well as indoor ones. As we near the house, you seem surprised by how small it looks. But I explain that this is deliberate since the indoor space spills out into the outdoor, and that many of the functions that occupy ones life can take place there.

You give me a mock grimace: There is such a thing as winter, you know. And I'm not the sort that considers freezing a form of entertainment.

I smile: Just hang on...

You nod resignedly, apparently deciding that this tour is obviously going to be largely irrelevant for you but that you might just as well be pleasant and go along for the ride. After all, the air is fresh and clean, the temperature ideal, and it's a lovely day to be tromping around outdoors.

We walk over to the south side of the house, which is flanked by an attached green house. There are pungent herbs and beds of succulent greenery inside – New Zealand spinach, I think. At that moment Jo, who is the farmer in the family, steps into the greenhouse with a bucket of something she pours on the plants. She dries her hands on her overalls, and introduces herself.

She picks up on our interest in the spinach. It looks nothing like the spinach in the supermarket, you comment, but it sure looks vibrant and full of life.

It tolerates the heat of the greenhouse well, she explains, and by winter comes in really handy, when green stuff is at a premium. It makes a yummy cream soup. Then it mostly gives way to lots of little pots of starter plants by early spring.

Jo leads us beyond the house toward a chicken coop. There's a flock scratching around and clucking happily. Jo checks the water dispenser and explains: The chickens are for laying, but when the little ones come along there are always fryers to cook, and the hens are routinely moved around over the garden plots to eat the insects and weed seeds before a new area is planted. Here we can grow some things in the late winter and early spring outdoors, and others during the summer, and get in a fall crop of greens as well.

In back is a small "field". Though not as large as would normally be used for such crops, it can, she explains, be overplanted three times a year with a series of grains and beans. Some plots are too small to allow this, but this one is ample. You can, if you wish, grow enough grain and beans [*] for a family of four to six.

You ask where the tiller and mowers are, but she says there are none: This is a well-established operation, and the earth is in prime condition. All you need to do is push back the mulch and plant what you want. The grain patch is also

[*] A combination of grain and beans is the common denominator of many, if not most, of the diets traditional among healthy populations. It supplies a complete protein, and serves a major protein source, even when small amounts of animal foods are also consumed.

a no-till area, there is little you need to do but cut it with a scythe, and after shaking off the grain, throw the stalks back, sow on top of that for the next crop, and voila!

What about weeds?

Well, we don't let most weeds go to seed, and the ones there are, the chickens eat most of when they are in this area. With little seed for them to grow from there are very few. Sometimes that's even a problem, she laughs – at least for William, my partner—since a lot of the weeds are useful as herbal remedies, or for salads, and so forth, so that the ones that do grow, he generally uses up, and he goes foraging down the road to find more!

We see apple, pear, plum, cherry, fig, and persimmon trees. There are blue-berry bushes, chestnuts, and heart nuts. A couple of oaks in a corner, she says, yield a generous crop of non-bitter acorns, which are incorporated into breads and breakfast cereal to give them a richer flavor and to add the minerals that the trees pull up from deep in the soil. In the far corner of the lot, there is a pond that has visible ducks and, she claims, invisible fish that are edible.

Ducks, chickens, fruit trees…I can't imagine how much work it must take to take care of all this, you sigh.

Well, actually, there is a bit to learn about how to handle it all, Jo confesses. But you would be surprised how low-maintenance it is now. The chickens need some protection from marauding canines, and the so do the ducks, but they both need minimal feeding because they forage for themselves most of the year. The fruit trees and bushes are chosen for their disease resistance and their suitability for this area, so manage quite well with nothing more than yearly applications of fertilizer now that they are established.

I guess I like to be outside, she continues, and even in the winter I enjoy my half hour of chores in the morning feeding the chickens and ducks. But really, the amount of time I have to be working outside is no more than a few hours a week on the average. It sure was a *lot* more when we were just getting this all set up: clearing, planting, weeding, but that has dropped off to very little now.

How much of my food could be generated here? you ask.

Well, if you are happy without red meat and dairy, and if you are willing to do a bit of canning or dehydrating of your surpluses to use during the winter, and if you are content with a diet of fish, fowl, salads, veggies, grains and beans, fruits, berries, and nuts, you could conceivably live on nothing more than what you generate on this half acre [*] – not counting the occasional chocolate bar, the vanilla extract, cardamom, turmeric, dates, and stuff like that, that you might want for an exotic touch here and there.

And the cost? you ask.

Cost? She echoes. You mean the selling price for the place?

No, I mean the fertilizers, pesticides, equipment, gardeners, and so forth. What does it add up to a year?

Mostly we've used chicken manure as fertilizer, plus compost we make. My pesticide use is limited to a few organic preparations of non-toxics, but most of those I've dropped as the little ecosystem here has settled into harmonious function. I still use a bit of discarded motor oil to do a dormant oil spray of the fruit trees in late winter, because some of the neighbors have sickly trees that draw insect pests.

I use almost exclusively hand tools, but on the occasion we need to till something, there is a tool co-op in the neighborhood, where we can rent or borrow a tiller or mower for a day. Would you like to see the inside?

Inside you meet her partner William, who's busy with his herbal preparations. William is an affable sort, bearded, slim, in his late forties. He shares with us that his passion is herbal remedies and flower essences – two modes of healing in which he is accomplished. He's brewing a flower essence of tiger lilies, as we talk. I ask what it is for. He laughs: Oh, it's for the wild feminine! When Jo looks up, he adds, with an innocent shrug: in *anyone*!

Jo is roughly the same age as William, but somewhat heavier. She's an avid cycler, and also the custodian of their vintage Volvo, which she's converted to ethanol. Curious about how to fix her bike, then, eventually, the car, she has developed a little repair business.

It started when I wondered if I could do the retrofit of the car to run on gasohol. We have a friend nearby who makes alcohol from whatever the local farmers can bring as a feedstock, she says. We have quite a bit of Jerusalem arti-

---

[*] A half acre is not an uncommon size for the outer suburban areas of most US cities. While conventional thinking holds that much more land than that is necessary to house and feed 3 or 4 people, such calculations are not based on intensive, organic farming. *www.pathtofreedom.com* details the production of up to 6000 lbs of food per year with over 350 vegetables, herbs, fruits, and berries from one tenth of an acre (the lot is one fifth acre, the gardening area – lot minus the footprint of the house and garage—one tenth. See also *www.youtube.com/dervaes#p* a for a short video on the Path to Freedom urban homestead.) Thus our half acre site in this chapter is actually quite generous.

chokes, which grow like weeds around here. We combine them with Mary and Nance's crop and have enough to do a run of ethanol. Since we don't do a lot of driving – mostly we bike to town and to visit neighbors – we can last the better part of the year with the ethanol we get from that. It's quite a little savings.

One by one we've eliminated many of the ordinary expenses a family has. So we can make do on minimal income. You might say we are, in large part, supported by Gaia, Jo laughs. William has his herb and flower essence consultations, and between the two, we can do pretty well. I could go back to bikes, too, and he could sell more tinctures, but we want to keep it simple. Josh, our older son, is a top notch geek, and for the last 3 years, he has done a little computer business – he can take a pile of discarded junk and set you up a system in a flash – so we are flush as far as outside income. Fortunately taxes around here are rock bottom.

They show us the house: It is small and yet it has an elegance that seems to come from everything serving its function in a simple, matter of fact way. The living room is Japanese in spirit, with mostly low seating and cushions, and a view onto the greenhouse. The kitchen has an alcohol burning two-unit stove top, and a sink with water piped from a roof rainwater catchment barrel for dish washing. We filter the water we drink, William explains.

The furniture is oak and butternut, made by a friend from trees they had cut from the lot. The hearth is local stone. There's a wood stove for heat, though it's really just for back-up because the house is solar/geothermal.

What does that mean? you ask.

It's called a loop house, Jo offered.

Loop?

Yes, it's also known, more technically, as a "double envelope" or "double shell" house. That's because the structure of the house is like two envelopes surrounding the main living space. Between those two envelopes or shells is the "loop" space. This includes the attached greenhouse on the south side of the house, the crawl space underneath, the attic above, and some sort of passage or conduit for airflow on the north (*see Figure 6*). In our case it's a double wall on the north, and since it's a small house, that was not a big expense.

So the air flows around the living space?

Exactly. If you think of the house as a cube, it's merely a matter of connecting those four sides of that cube – or rather connecting the envelope space around those four sides — attic on top, greenhouse on the south, crawl space underneath, and air passageway on the north.

And why do you do that?

To wrap it in warm — or warmer — air than what's outside in the winter (and cooler in the summer). It works in two phases: During the day when the sun is shining on the greenhouse the warm air rises, flows through the attic and then, as the colder air on the north side sinks in its envelope, the air drops down into the crawl space. There, it deposits some of the heat that it had picked up in the greenhouse, then reenters the sunny space and repeats its cycle.

So the ground under the house gets warmer?

Yes, though the temperature of the earth in the winter here will already naturally hover around 45-50 degrees Fahrenheit. But with the greenhouse heated air flowing over it, that temperature rises, and it becomes a "heat sink."

At night, the process reverses: The greenhouse, because of all the glass, cools quicker than the house, and the colder air drops directly down into the crawl space. This pulls air from the attic into the greenhouse, "driving" the loop in the opposite direction from how it flows during the day. During night-

Figure 6: The Double Envelope House, A Solar/Geothermal Design

time, then, the heat stored in the crawl space during the day is picked back up, and keeps the green house from cooling off as much as it otherwise would.

With this sort of "winter wrap," and with the heating that comes from the sun – which is lower in the sky in the winter – shining into the house thru the windows that separate the greenhouse from the main living space, the house can stay warm with no additional heat beyond our warm bodies, the cook stove and electric lights. That may not be true during an unusually cold spell with cloudy days, but that's pretty rare.

So the greenhouse stays at a sort of intermediate temperature?

Yes, we like to say that there are three climates here: the outside climate, the loop climate, and the inside climate. Outside around here it can get as low as 10 degrees below zero. In the loop we maintain a subtropical climate: a lowest low that is still above freezing.

That's why I see bougainvilla there.

Yep, when I'm in south Florida, or, say, Santa Barbara, California, I can buy plants at the nurseries that are right at home in the greenhouse. And, of course, the temperature of the main part of the house – the third climate—remains a comfortable 66 to 74 degrees all winter.

But what happens in the summer?

Up to a point, the loop flow can also cool. The hot air pulled over the crawl space floor – the earth – is cooled and the envelope air is tempered. But during really hot spells, we open the windows at the top of the greenhouse so the overheated air is kicked out to the outside. In the process, cooler air is pulled from the shaded north through the windows on that side of the house via the even cooler crawl space to replace it.

It's ingenious. But is it expensive to run?

How do you mean?

I mean the fans, or whatever moves the air.

There are no fans. It is what's called a passive system. No moving parts, nothing to break down.

But you have to be thinking about what to open when….

In the summer, yes….But we don't mind thinking about it. Tending it is like keeping up a sacred space. It's like a little spiritual shrine for us.

Shrine?

Yes, it's neither purely solar nor purely geothermal, though at times it does derive heat – or cooling—from the earth. So it's a collaborative creation of the sun and the ground, Heaven and Earth.

I can't resist stepping in at this point: Here's the tantric marriage, I explain. She and He dancing together to provide the space for human life. He brings down light and She grounds it and makes it suitable for plants and animals. The house is a sort of vortex of their blending influences.

You, remembering the tantric quest that led you to me and to this visit, contemplate the equation: house as shrine…

Then, perhaps, looking for other linkages, you ask about the fridge: there is a chest freezer but no fridge. Why did you make that choice? you query.

William laughs. That's not a freezer. We don't have one. We dry stuff and can other things, and there is a root cellar you enter over there, where we store apples, potatoes, carrots, rutabagas, and sour kraut, through the winter, and other things short term. But that is a chest fridge. It takes less energy than an upright one, which loses all its cold air when you open it. This one is big, because it is super insulated, and with it, and no AC or electric heat, we keep our electricity usage really low. In fact, the photovoltaic panels that we put up almost always – except if we have a long run of cloudy days,—generate enough power to sell back into the grid. We practically never pay an electric bill, and periodically get cash from the power company.

The bathrooms have composting toilets, and the roof top catchment from the house and outbuildings supplies most of the water each one needs, unless it is a very dry summer. Then they use water from our city hookup. Besides, all the shower, washing machine and sink water – the "greywater"—goes through a gravel bed and into the garden or through another sand bed and into the fishpond. In a bind, a small solar pump could send it back up to the house for the yard, or even, with enough filtration, to use in the house, but we've never needed to do that.

You've thought of everything, you comment. And the house has the mellow feel of simplicity and ….contentment.

William laughs. Yes, I suspect that it comes from a lot of the finish work—the wood and stone—being hand done. And from the fact that there have been many happy times here…But I'm sure that Jo can give you more – shall we say "philosophical" reasons.

Jo blushes. Well, I do teach permaculture.

What? you ask.

Permaculture. That's the art and science of setting up a home and land this way. It's the combination of a lot of practical knowledge from many cultures translated into a modern semi-urban or rural setting.

So why do you think the place feels so mellow and pleasant?

Well, I don't think that it's an accident….It was engineered to put us in touch with Nature…to feel Her presence all around and inside the house. If we're out of touch with Her, then life on planet Earth becomes something other than what we were designed to experience. Research shows that when people don't experience the changing temperatures, the changes in humidity, the shifts in light from day to night, when we don't feel the breeze, the Schwann waves that are often filtered out by roofs, or don't smell the odors of soil and plants and animals, we start to lose our vitality.

But even more than that, the way we live here, we are working *with* Nature. Not forcing our technology and our synthetic objects and wastes down Her throat. We are asking what She wants to grow, and out of that range of plants selecting what can also sustain us. We are caring for Her – in an ongoing practical way. We lovingly care for Her body – "trimming her nails," so to speak—as we cut Her trees, plant others, re-vegetate washed out gullies, or create more "edges," with wavy interfaces between water and grass, so that more species will flourish.

You look skeptical: But if you really wanted to respect Nature, wouldn't you leave her totally alone – allow her to be the wilderness she wants to be?

Jo looked thoughtful for a moment. There have been environmentalists who think that way – especially some of the urban dwellers, who feared the loss of the last vestiges of wild nature – and some of them even see humans as "a scourge upon the earth." But most of us in the Permaculture movement see Nature as incomplete without us. We believe that we are an integral part of the ecosystem. We think that the goal of making wilderness preservations is too limited: A few preserves, like museums, where people can't go or they will ruin it….That's sad.

Instead, we aspire to find our rightful role as *a part* of Nature. Historians are rewriting the story of this continent now [*], and instead of accepting the old notion that it was inhabited largely by small groups of mostly nomadic tribes, they are revising the estimates upwards dramatically, finding evidence that the Americas were home to tens of millions of people. And those people even tended the forests in many and skilled ways. In fact, the Europeans who first came were stunned by the great cathedral-like forests with their huge trees and open spaces. This is now thought to be the result of many indigenous traditions and practices, such as controlled burns, for after some decades and the epidemics brought by the invaders, huge majorities of the natives died off, and the Europeans who came after that found the forests to be tangled webs of undergrowth and crowded trees that could not reach maturity.

This is not to claim that we have found the ultimate way to live with nature. We are constantly learning. And there are new and exciting approaches, such as "edible forest gardening," which intends to blaze a trail into the cultivation and re-creation of intact forest ecologies using the vast array of edibles that the world offers and that are now available to people everywhere [**]. This could recapture, if not every detail, at least the spirit of both allowing Her to become the primeval forest She loves to be, and to restore men and women to their rightful place as strategic stewards of Nature.

Again, feeling compelled to reinforce that with a tantric gloss, I interject: *Spanda*, without tapas, is doomed to drain her energy away in random habits. She needs Him. And we are Him, in this context. When we patiently tend Her, take out a bush here, or plant a new species of tree there, with thought and perceptiveness – *discrimination*, Shiva would say—we make it possible for Her to blossom in Her full glory. And the abundance of that nourishes us. Then we are no longer a burden or destructive force for Her. Instead we have become Her protectors and cohabiters. It is another prime example of the outer marriage that, when cultivated, supports and catalyzes our inner marriage.

You brighten, beginning to see, I suspect, why I dragged you out of your house to look at a farm.

All the things we do could be seen as exploiting the earth for our needs, explains Jo. But they're *not*, because we don't force Her. We are supporting Her in doing what She does, and then merely partaking of the bounty that flows out of that. When we relate to Her that way, it is Her pleasure that nurtures us. We could look at each piece of what we do in a day and think of it as an act of devotion, as a ritual of worship of the Goddess: Each time we pull back

[*] see 1491
[**] See the two volume work titled *Edible Forest Gardening*

mulch and nudge seeds into Her body, each time we clip shrubs, or remove dead limbs, we adorn and festoon Her body so as to honor and delight Her.

When we sit outside the kitchen after supper, Jo continues, and Josh plays his guitar while the sun sinks and colors the sky deep reds, and the breeze cools, it is though we are sitting in Her lap, a sensual experience of deepest pleasure. We come more fully into our bodies when we relate more fully to Her body.

Moreover, the garden, the herb beds, the stone and wood surfaces, the overhanging vines on the arbor that shades the porch, the bees, the butterflies – we have butterflies! They are more and more rare in the pesticide-laden fields of agribusiness – everything here adds up to a different aesthetic: simple, determined by Nature. The lines of house and garden follow the patterns of nature's curves—its rises and falls. We don't carve up the land with heavy machinery to level it for a parking lot, we work with the contours that are already there. It sings with delight. It wants to manifest Her. It is Her manifesting Herself: Her whimsy, Her unpredictability, Her ebbs and Her flows, Her outrageous combinations of colors and fragrances.

I feel moved to pipe up: This is what we might call "the inner marriage externalized," the alchemical principle put to work. The outer relationship, our relation to Nature, we are coaxing along, living its purification, correcting the grievous errors our collective actions on the planet have perpetrated against Her. We are thinking globally about the change that needs to happen and acting locally to manifest that change. We are harnessing our own inner marriage to that outer one, and we feel the change within ourselves. We caress the land, and the She within us whispers to Him, Ahh…that feels delicious, and He smiles and His breath quickens.

One might think this is just a dinky little semi-urban "farmlet," rather silly and not impressive, where clever and lazy people have dug in to avoid an honest job, and to live a irresponsible, neo-hippy life of irrelevance. But not so. It is a bold and radical approach to a planetary crisis, and it is a gutsy spiritual practice that touches the deepest currents of longing for unification with the Infinite. It is a deft disengagement from a deadening consumerism that is the true terrorist of the 21st century. It is an eloquent renunciation of violence and a sensual act of love.

Jo beams as she absorbs my soliloquy.

As we are bidding our hosts goodbye, you acknowledge: I am charmed, overwhelmed, humbled by what I don't know – so *much* that I didn't know that I didn't know! I am smitten, and intrigued. I need to think about this possibility, and I will call....

But, you add, I have one question: Why would you ever think of selling this lovely little paradise?

Jo, smiles and leans on the heavy kitchen table: It was a big decision. But we hanker after more open spaces....and besides, this spot is happy now. It radiates health and high energy. We – I for sure – have a commitment to healing the land. That's part of the permaculture credo. I need to shift my attention to one of the countless parcels of land that are not so happy: One of the places that has been abused, where Nature is suffering from Post Traumatic Stress Syndrome. Where trees need to be planted, gullies stopped, the soil rebuilt, and the vitality returned to the land. We know how to do that, and we love doing it.

As I take you back to your present home, I reflect on the visit: Tantra, we like to say, is an embodied spirituality. Embodiment means integrating the teachings, the techniques, the explorations and experiments into your total physical/mental/emotional and spiritual being. If the way you live, the space you create, your relationship to your food and where it comes from, your use of the earth's resources, your relationship to Gaia who feeds and clothes and shelters you – and whose fluids run through your veins – are all unconscious, indifferent, and damaging to the web of life of which you are a part, then that's not embodied. It doesn't matter that you breathe when you're having sex, or that you say a mantra sometimes. It doesn't add up to Tantra. Tantra is about the integration of the whole, the conscious weaving together of the fabric of life.

What you saw today is an ashram – a place where life itself is a worship, and the energies of those present is dedicated to bringing spirit into flesh, and bringing embodiment to spirit. The more completely that pervades your life, the fuller your tantric experience. To overlook the nature of your home and its surroundings is too unconscious to qualify as Tantra.

As I stop in front of your place, I turn to look at you and explain: The reason I took you there was so that the contrast of what you saw today and the way the world is working will hit you squarely in the eye. The vast majority of what is happening in the world today is not like that. Land is not treated with respect, nor are plants cultivated to nurture those you love. On the contrary food production is impersonal, mechanized, horribly inefficient – using ten times as much energy to produce as it yields, and a total failure when it comes to the taste and the nutrition that it offers. It is almost possible to call it fake food. The plants that produce it are so nearly devoid of vitality that they are mercilessly preyed on by insects and microbes that are justified in assuming that the plants should be broken down and recycled.

Water is not respected and conserved and revered as the life-giving sacrament that flows through all living things and unites us. It is regarded as a resource to be exploited, or even worse, as a necessary commodity that can be controlled and used to extort the last pennies from those who are most unfortunate. Our homes have become plastic monsters bloated, hollow, and empty of life, inhabited by only one or two or three of us, who are never there, as we work long hours to pay off a mammoth mortgage. And if we have found a way to bring in that much money, we eat out, go away every weekend, and seldom have the nerve to face the absurdity and meaninglessness of the McMansion we have saddled ourselves with.

Even the air we breathe is toxic – so many chemicals have been churned out to produce the plastic junk we cart home in our oversized vehicles. And so we take another – often just one of many we use—mind-altering pill at night, perhaps to avoid thinking of the toll our hyper consumption takes on the environment and on the masses of off shore slaves that make our madness possible.

The violence both overt and implicit in this assault on life and the Earth is difficult to fully grasp. Yet it is so fundamental to our social system that it has become almost invisible to us. We can no longer see it or, rather, it seems normal to us. Just like the domestic violence dynamic, no one can understand where it comes from. What we see just looks like a normal household, and then the violence erupts. It does so, because it is woven into the set up from the get-go. It's inherent in the nature of the distorted form of the Masculine that is leading the way. And that, that twisted version of the Masculine is us – all of us, men *and* women – when it comes to humans relating to Nature. We are the Masculine, and She is the victim of the violence.

That was a short rant, I smile. I figured I could avoid a long one by showing you what is possible, not focusing on what is with us now on a large scale. When you see how we can live, and how much joy it can bring, you may begin to sense the level of violence that surrounds you, and you may understand why our current approach to the environment might be termed "Egging Kali On." If we keep pushing in the direction we've been going, I suspect that She will be obliged to rise up and brush away the nonsense, opening the way for us to return to sanity.

CHAPTER 4

The Social/Political/Economic Scene

Perceiving Institutionalized Violence
~ or Forms generated as a result of fearing Kali,
and: New Forms on the horizon that ride on Kali's energy! ~

I am explaining to Steve Schwartzberg why I'm standing at a sink with a faucet that doesn't yield water (in a cabin in an Ecovillage) pouring rainwater from a plastic milk jug, to slowly massage the food residue from each dish and rinse it down the pseudo sink into a bucket beneath.

Some folks would say that I'm simply crazy, and that it's silly to tolerate such unnecessary inconvenience, I tell him, as he peers over my shoulder with a knitted brow. But I have meditated on this at length and see how much the "conveniences" we find so essential are obtained at the expense of working long hours at jobs we often care little for. By living this way I can eliminate that – and have more free time even though it takes me longer to wash my dishes.

But then it's not all about me either. What are the repercussions out in the world – across the globe, really – of wresting from it the resources – not to mention the labor – that we need to be able to "enjoy" these conveniences (a sort of post-globalization addendum to Thoreau's argument, I suppose), and how does it also (back to me) affect me if I collude in that rape and pillage? Heart attacks (closed heart)? Cancer (the embodiment of malignant growth gone wild)?[*]

There was a time, I suppose, when the "haves" could live comfortably in their affluence with the "have nots" tucked safely away in some remote part of the city, the country, or the world. But we have spoiled that arrangement with information technology. Now it takes a grim determination to avoid knowing the costs of our wastefulness. We must steer clear of certain websites, magazines, and television channels, where sweat-shops with grinding child labor abuses are turned inside out for us to see. We must stick our fingers in our ears, squeeze our eyelids shut, and say, "La, la, la, la, la, ..." loudly and almost continuously. While some of us are so determined to avoid knowing the truth that we will go to such lengths, others are giving in and getting the message.

The subject is not pleasant. I am not sure that my "contract" with you, the reader, includes broaching such distasteful matters. When I was growing up in the midst of my mother's extended tribe in South Carolina, we were frequently reminded of the customary rule: there are two things that you don't talk about without risking severe blow-ups: religion and politics. Of course, we did it anyway, and the family – of largely Irish descent – reveled in the blow-ups. So, bowing to family karma, perhaps, I am about to talk of both those forbidden topics in this and the next chapter.

In these last two chapters we are working our way toward closing with a consideration of spirituality of the tantric variety. Perhaps an *embodied* spirituality has to work more directly with and be more observant of the nitty-gritty world of greed and corruption, of politics and economics – in order to fully own the lower chakras and consciously participate in the reconfiguration of them.

In any case, my overriding intent here is to look squarely at the major facets of our contemporary lives – not averting our gaze at any point – to identify the threads of violence woven through it, and to understand how to liberate *spanda*, i.e., to free the Yang Feminine from her longstanding solitary confinement, so that we can launch a new way of being on the planet that is joyful, free, and creative.

[*] After forty years of practicing holistic medicine, and contemplating the relationship of the diseases I have seen and the psychosocial pressures that seem to push them into expression, I feel increasingly that heart disease is at least partially a result of the "closing of the heart" that is necessary to live with the massive violence that is done to Nature and third world populations in order for us to "enjoy" the "affluence" that we have become accustomed to. In a somewhat comparable way (but via a distinct mechanism), our preoccupation with "growth" – more dollars circulating, more and larger cars, houses, more mining, petroleum, land clearing – without regard to the impact of this on the health of the host, Gaia, eventually spills over into physical expression and begins to be replicated by malignant tumors in our own physical bodies.

For it is violence that has crushed Her. i.e., as per our working definition, violence is the crushing of Spanda, the abrogation of Her power (think "Girl Interrupted"). If we can come to identify clearly the violence and grasp how it operates, then we are already liberating Spanda/Shakti. For as we see the violence clearly, it must wither; it cannot withstand the light. It operates and thrives in darkness. Therefore, we must be turning away, averting our gaze, for it to continue. The triumph of "good over evil" that lives so vibrantly in our mythos, is not, in its essence a moral victory. It is a victory of consciousness, of bringing the descending light of consciousness into the darkness to clarify the truth and to make us aware that no force, human or otherwise, can abrogate our power – without our unconscious collusion. In other words, there is no violence that is not collective. My failure to own and exercise my personal power is my contribution to the violence that surrounds me.

This is the message of the story and image of Kali. She is the unrestrainable. She is the power unleashed that clears away everything in Her path. She is the truth of the deepest archetypal infrastructure of our being. We cannot be disempowered without surrendering Her, surrendering our Yang Feminine. And, of course, denying Her, exiling Her, refusing to acknowledge that She lives in us, is the ultimate giving in – giving up—the ultimate self-disempowerment.

So what is painful about looking at the nexus of violence that we call home on planet Earth, is that it is of our making – i.e., that we each and all participate in its origination and its promulgation. And what is reassuring, if frightening, is that we cannot exile Her indefinitely. Eventually, She will be fed up and She will return with a vengeance, She will rise again and obliterate all negation of Herself.

It's all a question of how long we want to wait to address the violence. At this point, we hesitate because it feels overwhelming, since it has worked its way, invasively, through the entire fabric of our society and its institutions.

From one point of view, the present structures of our society might be seen as an accumulation of our piecemeal accommodations of greed and predation. We have lived for some decades now with a casual consensus that "greed is good." Why, it will motivate us, drive the market, bring all kind of marvelous growth to our economy and bear us all away on a tsunami of "economic prosperity." Won't it? Meanwhile, "on the ground," as they say, it ain't looking all that great.

In fact, greed is performing pretty much the way we might have expected it to: Some are accumulating wealth of absurd proportions, while others are living in tent camps around our cities. Starvation in our global economic "colonies" has boomed and in poor countries where there are scraps of earnings available from mining the rare elements we need to construct our electronic toys, civil wars rage and barbaric killing reigns. We tsk tsk at the incivility of the dark masses, and remain "practical" about what to put our investments in. (That means wherever they increase the fastest.)

Our investment advisors don't advise us that the money that we are sending is used to produce weapons, for example, that are marketed to both sides of the civil wars we foment, nor that such dark manipulations are considered unworthy of comment. In the unlikely event that some brash young journalist (if indeed there are any left) decides there is a story in it, the corporate sponsored media close ranks and kill it. There is a mild contempt for those who would bring up such unsavory matters and contaminate the common decency of our social discourse.

On another front, the food industry serves up the most disgusting, devitalized, and toxic selection of pseudo foods imaginable — accurately characterized as "Frankenfoods," by a growing opposition. Health plummets as bodies bloat and we develop what is probably the most alarming epidemic of obesity ever seen on the planet. Yet somehow no one questions the legitimacy of using advertising to push such dangerous products, or the legal underpinnings of businesses that would allow commercial interests to destroy the health and well being of a whole nation. We may shake our heads and consider for a moment what a sad state of affairs it represents, but it is, we sigh collectively, after all, business. "And every thing they are doing is legal."

Yet the damage done to physical health and mental capacities is obvious. This effectively disables the clarity and vitality that are necessary to experience and manifest ones creativity, ones inherent spanda.

The above examples are only a few representative ones. I cite them to indicate the pervasiveness of the violence that has come to be accepted as normal. There are countless other examples that surround us on every side: The financial control of elections with private funds, the buying of legislators by lobbyists and their employers, the suppression of technology that would challenge the profits of the fossil fuel industries, the assassination of union leaders by paramilitaries hired by American corporations in the far flung production plants abroad.

It would, indeed, require a very large book even to list the current major such abuses — the ones that affect large numbers of people and generate huge profits for the perpetrators. The film "the Corporation" details the characteristics of the current business model that both allow and ensure its violence. It makes a convincing case for the diagnosis of the corporation (an "individual" under prevailing interpretations of the law), as psychopath/sociopath. We've recently seen our financial industry driven off a cliff by its managers, who enshrined greed and violence to amass mountains of money that was acquired unethically (and often illegally, even according to a legal system that has become distorted by legislative roll-backs and behind-closed-doors tampering).

Additional glaring examples are obvious in practically any field of endeavor we might happen upon. Let me mention two more, health and education:

Our system of medicine is now profit-driven, and has long been violent in its fundamental principles – it subdues the crises of the body with toxic medications rather than working *with* Nature to guide It through the journey of healing of which It is capable. [*]

Our system of education is, on close analysis, also largely dominated by violence. Instead of working with children to cultivate their spontaneity, and to help them identify their uniqueness, the emphasis is on control and conformity. This is now widely enforced through the use of drugs – an estimated 20-30% of boys [**] in some highly competitive New York schools are on medication for "Attention Deficit Disorder." Such brutal crushing of self-expression is what destroys all awareness of the power—the shakti—that is their birth right. No wonder they find it difficult to locate the Yang Feminine within themselves, to find their way, to feel the passion of their unique talents and capacities.

When these forms of violence are layered over the violence we learn to do to our bodies (*see Chapter 1*), the violence built into our family dynamics and personal relationships (*Chapter 2*), the violence inherent in our way of relating to the environment (*Chapter 3*), then you will begin to appreciate how ubiq-

---

[*] Even according to data published by the Journal of the American Medical Association, the industry mouthpiece, more than 100,000 persons a year die from the use of the standard medications. And these figures are excluding those deaths from overdoses, errors in prescription, and drug interactions. They are also limited to deaths in hospital, excluding those occurring outside. The total could be twice that, or more.

[**] Boys are usually prescribed such medications at more than twice the rate at which girls are. These figures have to be estimates, since no good data has been collected (or has been kept secret by the drug companies) since 2005. Figures from then showed a nearly 10% rate for boys, with a steady increase of close to 12% per year. I spoke with one respected professor of psychiatry who has published on the subject and who felt that use has continued to rise briskly since 2005, and that it is particularly high where parents are eager to push their children to get into prestigious universities. That corresponds to my own clinical impression.

uitous violence is. We might go so far as to say that violence has become the core "value" – or at least, the core *modus operandi*—of our planetary culture.

It may not be an exaggeration to say that the origin of most of these violent trends can be traced to a fear of, and attempt to, control and suppress – even to obliterate – the unpredictable power we call shakti, and most especially Her remedial, avenging, extreme alter ego, Kali. It is She, who is feared. It is She who must be kept locked away from sight, and prevented from coming into play. It is She who will threaten the rule of the slave holders. It is She that can "ruin everything," bring down the system, cause the grievous loss of "everything we have worked for," and humiliate those men and women who are thoroughly brainwashed by, and under the control of, the distorted, impotent, rageful, and fearful Yang Masculine that currently rules the roost.

It is to keep Her in exile that he perpetrates his desperate violence.

That violent determination to keep Her out of sight has become hard and brittle. Like a coat of concrete stuck to the earth's surface, it is cracking and giving way now. She can no longer be constrained, even by concrete. The parking lots, once geometrically perfect and brightly self-assured, are fracturing, fragments pushed askew by Her brewing, boiling power below. And through the crevices spring green sprouts, weeds, grass, and wildflowers, poking their heads up with fresh optimism.

Emerging Revolutions I (Economic)

It's Tuesday night – cookout/potluck night—and we are under a canvas canopy next to a century old log barn on the edge of a creek in our Ecovillage in the mountains of western North Carolina. We've about finished a meal of homegrown bounty, when our presenters for the after-supper happening step forward. They have come from "town" (Asheville) and are here to tell us about the Local Exchange Trading System, LETS [*], they have been a part of creating there.

It's an online system. When you offer goods or services to someone else in the network, they credit you via the website. When they do the same, the recipient credits them. Each participant/member strives to maintain a zero balance. So far, they explain, in their 400 member group, there has been no one who has had to be approached for going too far into negative territory.

[*] See Local Exchange Trading Systems, Wikipedia

Why? we ask. Because we have gatherings, because lots of us know each other. Because it's more of a community than a business arrangement. If it grows beyond 4-500 members, we close it. Others will need to start a new group in their locale....

Perched on the edge of the sturdy rough-sawn serving table, they answer question after question until it's so dark we can barely see each other. Do people stick with it? Is it a stable arrangement?

Some groups thought that participation was waning but discovered that members just quit recording their transactions. They get into the swing of feeling when they need to offer something to balance what they've received, and just skip the online data entry. They smiled: That's why we sometimes call LETS "a gift economy with training wheels."

A gift economy [*] was still in evidence around me when I was a child in rural South Carolina. Members of our 60-odd strong family were constantly visiting and most often brought baskets of peaches, or squash, or butter beans or corn or whatever they had lots of – and whether you grew it or bought it, you always aimed for extra, so that you could pass it on. When you needed help, you rarely called a repairman, you asked someone in the family who knew how to lend a hand. Baby sitters were unknown, what with aunts and grandparents and cousins everywhere.

Though such arrangements may be easy to dismiss as both minor and impractical, Sharon Astyk, in her entertaining and compelling account of stepping out of consumer culture [**], observes that much of the world functions outside the "formal economy," i.e., that which is transacted in money and which supplies the statistics on which we base our economic theories. She notes that in Africa 25 years ago researchers began to notice that there was no economic explanation of how the majority of the population survived.

"They didn't own land. They didn't seem to have any assets. According to conventional economics they should have died of hunger long ago, but they survived. To understand this, researchers looked at how these people actually lived, rather than economic models. They found that their way of life was completely the opposite of how a human being in an industrial society survives. They didn't have a job, pension, steady place to work or regular flow of income. Families held a range of occupations from farming and selling in the market to doing odd jobs or handicrafts."

[*] See Wikipedia
[**] *Depletion and Abundance, Life on the New Home Front.* Gabriola Island, BC: New Society Publishing.

Their aim was to live simply and provide for their basic needs, rather than to realize monetary profit. Labor was used within the family rather than to earn wages. [*]

Astyk says that studies such as the above, duplicated all over the world, indicate that currently something like three quarters of the global workforce is involved in this "informal" economy (of which much is "gift" based). She suggests that we might regard the formal, monetary, economy as merely a *supplement* to the informal one – an adjunct that can be whittled away as we discover ways to move more of our transactions into the informal economy, which is largely immune to the blights that can ravage the financial world.

Why this is so important, and how it is related to questions of fear, violence, and environmental degradation is explained by Thomas Greco, most recently in his current book, *The End of Money and the Future of Civilization*. Greco details how our North American (and now Global) monetary system has painted us in a corner: In our present banking system, money enters circulation via the issuance of debt [**]. When you take out a loan, the money that comes to you is created (by an arrangement between the Treasury Department, the Federal Reserve and the Banks) de novo. Unfortunately, you must not only repay this debt, you must pay interest as well. No money is created for that.

As a result, there is insufficient money in circulation for all borrowers to repay their debts with interest. What results is a fierce competition for available funds [***]. Someone must default. While this explains some of the incentive for this practice (as set up by the Banks, working collectively, who come into ownership of the collateral put up by the defaulting borrower), it is not a sustainable system. Interest compounded means debt compounded, so that the collective debt eventually balloons out of control, whereupon the system begins to collapse.

---

[*]   *www.archive.newscientist.com/secure/article/article.jusp?rp=1&id=mg1*

[**]   Actual physical minted currency is but a tiny portion of the "money" in circulation. The vast majority is in the form of bank account balances, referred to as "deposits" but in fact nothing more than accounting data.

[***]   Though we generally consider normal rates of interest such a small percentage of a financial interaction that it would be unlikely to have significant economic impact, most financiers know otherwise. Greco illustrates the magnitude of compound interest and cumulative debt with a famous fable: An Oriental king is presented with a gift of a chessboard. Wishing to reciprocate, he asks what his guest would like in return. The request made is that the king supply an amount of rice on each of the following 64 days according to the number of squares on the chessboard: on the first day a single grain of rice on the first square, on the second, two grains, on the third, four grains, etc., doubling the amount each day. The king readily agrees assuming that the amounts will be trivial. Though at first, the quantity of rice is small, by the thirty second day, the cumulative amount is approximately 220 tons of rice, and by the 64th day it would be a billion times as much as that – much more rice than there is in the whole world!

While this meltdown can have dire financial consequences for those whose livelihoods and lives are locked into the monetary system, the repercussions run even deeper – whether or not the meltdown comes.

"… government and banking," Greco posits, "have colluded to create a political money system that embodies a 'debt imperative' that results in a 'growth imperative…'" It is only by "growth" that more money is loaned to expand businesses, and funds become available to pay off the prior loans. But in a vicious cycle like that of an addiction, the money gained by this method will create the need for even more money later.

"As borrowers compete with one another to try to meet their debt obligations in this game of financial 'musical chairs,' they are forced to expand their production, sales, and profits. They must take measures to enhance revenues and reduce costs by controlling both the markets in which they sell their products and those in which they buy their productive inputs, including labor. A major reason why corporations merge and consolidate and increase in size is so that they can exercise both greater political influence and greater market dominance." So that they won't be the ones squeezed out in the scramble for the funds to pay off debt and interest.

This desperate, relentless growth uses more and more of the natural resources of Nature and "forces environmental destruction, and rends the social fabric…. It creates economic and political instabilities that manifest in recurrent cycles of depression and inflation, domestic and international conflict, and social dislocation." [*]

Especially relevant to our analysis here—to the issues highlighted in the present book—is the fact that survival-based competition for a short supply of money virtually eradicates the possibility of a life organized around play and creativity. Survival and play, like oil and water, don't mix. There is no room here for the unpredictable spontaneity of the Yang Feminine (except, perhaps, in the smashing—Kali-style—of the whole game!)

We might imagine that those caught up in such a desperate struggle for survival must long for the reunion of the Yang Feminine with the Yang Masculine. That is to say, for the sort of adventurous goal directed action (phallic/Yang Masculine) that is firmly grounded in authentic *spanda* (the Yang Feminine). That happy confluence of the active parts of the human being is not avail-

---

[*]   These few brief paragraphs can hardly do justice to Greco's richly documented and well thought out critique of the current banking/monetary system. See annotated bibliography.

able in the Viagra-fueled pseudo-masculinity of the typical growth-at-all-costs business mindset.

Emerging Revolutions II (Socio-Political)

A primary thesis of this book is that we cannot budge from our planetary impasse until we bring into play our birthing capacity individually and collectively – in other words our ability to bring into manifestation genuinely new and creative solutions to the ills that plague us globally. That's what we have called *spanda*, a characteristic of the Yang Feminine.

So we might ask ourselves the question: what would a system of governance look like that has as its primary commitment the honoring and support of the Yang Feminine? I am not a political scientist, not even, in fact, very knowledgeable about the intricacies of civic affairs. But even I can see that our government feels remote, removed from my personal input. Our credo in the Ecovillage where I live is that more local is more manageable. In fact, a current buzz word in the permaculture world is "relocalization." Our own experiment with this challenge has led us to a commitment to consensus, and a sometimes bumpy exploration of modes of group process.

So I was intrigued when one of my sons took off for Oaxaca to hang out with Gustavo Esteva, a sort of guru of indigenous modes of governance in that remarkable state of Mexico, which has the largest concentration of Indian peoples in the country, and the only state where they represent a social majority. In fact, Oaxaca, the land of mystical art, boasts 16 native cultures, each with its own living language, traditions, cuisine, and culture.

The largest and most prominent, the Zapotec, is the most felt presence in the capitol city, and well down into the isthmus south of Oaxaca City. Esteva's grandmother was Zapoteca, and though he grew up in Mexico City in a home that attempted to eradicate the social liability of his Indian ancestry, he had fond memories of her and the village in Oaxaca where he went with her as a child. After a remarkable career that began with an executive position with IBM at the age of 22, that took him through a phase of Marxism and – caught up in the enthusiasm generated by Che Guevara—guerilla action, and that, in an amazing turnaround, landed him in the top echelons of the federal government, he left it all to return to a life of advocacy for the strong traditions of community, autonomy, and creativity of the Indians back in Oaxaca.

Esteva notes that through their patient, persistent efforts over many decades, the people of Oaxaca have been able to gradually secure the authority to officially instate their traditional forms of organization and governance in their communities. Of the 570 municipalities in the state, 412 elected to operate without political parties, without elections, but to constitute local governance according to traditional methods. "While violence and post electoral conflicts appeared in the municipalities where political parties continued to participate in local elections, none emerged in the municipalities where people were now able to follow traditional methods and get legal recognition for them."

Also, Esteva observes, unlike most indigenous peoples in most parts of the world, for whom land reform is the deeply needed though unattainable goal, "through continual struggle, the peoples of Oaxaca have acquired most of the arable land and all the forests. In that sense, agrarian reform has virtually come to an end: 7.4 million hectares of the 9.5 million hectares in the province are held under a form of social tenure; 73 percent of this is communal land."

Oaxacan native peoples now find themselves in the enviable position of frequently being able "to *bypass* the dominant institutions, seeing them as bureaucratic requisites of an alien and hostile world...." This has set the stage for an unparalleled demonstration of what can happen when the native cultures are free to create a modern adaptation of a traditional strong, earth-based community life. This can be critically instructive for those of us who have forgotten how to live in close connection with others. And it allows us to entertain some intriguing questions: Is it really possible to have sound community and personal freedom? Can *spanda* flourish when priorities are geared to the group welfare?

Esteva offers some clues: He places major emphasis on what he calls *autonomy*. This is the blending by a (very local and relatively small) group of people of their collective creative and spontaneous inspirations to continuously shape and re-shape the way in which they live together. This is possible only when they are minimally constrained by the overarching policies that apply to the area where they live. In other words, government at "county," state, and federal levels is limited to mere coordination, and plays a minor role in determining how things are done.

And how might this look in practice? Esteva shares a story about San Andres Chicahuaxtla, a little village of the Triqui nation, where the long and sometimes painful process of bringing this "post modern" renaissance of a reconfigured ancient culture into being is underway:

Don Marcos Sandoval is an elder who had been a leader of the village and who had fought to bring "the benefits of development" to his remote area of Oaxaca. Eventually, thanks to his efforts and that of the people, the village got electricity, a school, a health center, and a new municipal building "constructed with a lot of cement, the unmistakable sign of 'modernity.'" And Don Marcos remembers well the day when the road that reached the village was inaugurated.

His sons attended the school, and he struggled to enable them to continue their studies in a nearby town and as far as Mexico City. He believed, like all those of his generation that this would prepare them "to enrich the life of the village and create a better way of life for themselves."

Yet he was puzzled by the response of his sons when he complained that none of them ever came to help him in the *milpa* (the traditional plot of intercropped corn, beans, and squash, which is the heart of life for such native peoples) and bemoaned the loss of the knowledge of how to coax it into production. They reacted by blaming him: "Why did you send us to school, then?"

Meanwhile his sons were faced with their own increasing perplexity. "Day after day they asked themselves how they would use what they were learning at the school, which tended to alienate them from their village. The promises of comfort and prestige implicit in their formal education were unrelated to the reality around them in both the village and the city. They observed the increasing difficulties of those who already possessed diplomas, and they did not understand how some of them claimed that the miserable jobs they got in the cities were proof of success. Their discontent began to grow, taking different forms in each of them: Two abandoned their studies to start some initiatives in their own community, the remaining three followed the educational experience to the end and submitted their diplomas to the acid test."

One son, who became a teacher, got himself assigned to another Triqui village nearby. Since the government had abandoned the school, he created a new workshop style curriculum around learning skills that could be useful in the community. Eventually, only the "three R's" were left of the official program. Though in the end he was fired when the Ministry of Education discovered what he had done, by then his students were busily applying what they had learned, and his workshops were flourishing.

Another son, who also did teacher training, was faced with "a personal tragedy" when time came to return to the community: his wife refused to leave the city and come with him. He still brings his children to the village sometimes, but finds it difficult to detach them from their electronic games and to prevent them from wasting water. In any case, he and another of his brothers, who abandoned school, created "The House that Hosts Our Way," a center that promotes the revival and revision of traditional culture.

The two brothers interviewed all those who had held positions of authority in the community since the 1940's and found that those not attending school were more competent in everything the village needed than those who were schooled. So they explored alternative ways of learning for students. One project was the preparation of textbooks adjusted to regional conditions and written in Indian languages. The results were striking: instead of feeling impotent and uncomfortable when trying to help their children with homework about things they had no familiarity with, classes about local geography, for example, allow them to recover dignity and importance by revaluing their own knowledge.

One brother, who was slowly advancing in the hierarchy of responsibility in the community was selected to speak to the king and queen of Spain when they visited Oaxaca. He welcomed them to this ancient land "where different peoples conserve, coexist and resist with our own ways of life."

"We use this occasion to tell the Western world that our way of life has been essentially in community, with solidarity, with a profound respect for the land, our mother, which hosts us and nourishes us; that is why our heart is angry when we see how it is damaged, destroyed by ambition and greed, when it is denied to its ancestral owners, when the natural equilibrium is broken with so many industrial products.

We have been extensively studied from the view of the West, but we have not been understood. Its way of development, its civilization, its way of seeing the world, and its relation with nature are imposed on us, denying all the knowledge generated by our different peoples. We domesticated corn, our sacred food, which has given us our existence, and we are still improving it. Even so, every day, when an agronomist comes to the village, he tells us that the corn produced in their research centres is better; when we build our houses with our own knowledge and materials, an architect comes and says that to live in a dignified way we must have a house built with industrial materials; if we pray to our ancient gods, religious people come to tell us that our beliefs are superstitions. We can offer many other examples. That is why we want to tell the civilization of destruction that we offer our own civilization of conviviality, we only ask that they learn to see us."

When Esteva visited Chicahuaxtla, he had lunch in the "warm domain" of the mother of the Sandovals and wife of Don Marcos, Dona Refugio, whom we found sitting on the floor of her house, next to the open fire at the center of the room. We sat on very small benches around the fire, and we talked with her and her sons for several hours. She offered us, one by one, a great bowl of squash flower soup made from squash that grows in the *milpa*. More dishes cooked with other vetetables from the *milpa* came later, while we were talking about her reasons for living in the village and preserving her customs. She usually refused to leave Chicahuaxtla, although from time to time, she did accompany her husband on an errand to Oaxaca, as she had on many trips to Mexico City a few decades ago. Her sons had offered her a new stove and other comforts of modern houses, but she refused all of them. She even rejected a Lorena stove made of mud, which would have eliminated the open fire.

That open fire is the center of the warmest room of the house. Dona Refugio is there every day, at the center, surrounded by her family, talking with her sons or her husband, discussing personal matters or community affairs. That fire and Dona Refugio are the center of the conversation, and in fact the centre of family life/ and family life is the center of the community. The life in the community is in fact organized around those fires, in the center of the "kitchen" in the source of the *comida* [*]. The very essence of the *milpa* is here, not in the corn growing in the fields – the only element perceived by the agronomists. It is here, around the communal fire, in the heart of the family."

Esteva insists: "If I am to help us recover the soil under our feet, as I think we need to do, I cannot fail to allude to the cultures of the soil and to experiences that represent, in my view, a postmodern regeneration of tradition. I have never seen a nostalgic gaze in Dona Refugio. At some point in her life she felt the need to slow her pace and regain her own rhythm. Her sons did the same. They were able to take a look at the land promised by the modernizers, to smell what it would mean for their lives, and to decide to limit it. Dona Refugio can rise up from the open fire to enjoy the video filmed by her sons, and they can use this tool and other electronic gadgets. They do not live at the margin of "modernity," in a pre-modern world. But they are learning to limit modernity."

"By the open fire in the soil, in a situation continually denounced by many feminists, Dona Refugio presides over the life of her family and her community. Daily she becomes the centre of the house, and she cannot avoid a magnificent smile of satisfaction when her sons and the friends of her sons sit surrounding her after a meal and talk for several hours. She usually follows

[*] Food, in the context of Esteva's work: nurturance by the land where you are. See Esteva's "*Re-embedding Food in Agriculture*," Culture and Agriculture 48, 1994

every aspect of those conversations, intervenes whenever she finds it appropriate, and freely expresses her own views. Every day the magic of her fire brings before her eyes the incidents of a changing world, without taking her feet out of the ground."

A short time after his visit, Esteva relates, the Sandoval family had a solemn meeting.

"All the sons and their wives were there. They had come to make a very special decision: each of them would make a specific commitment to accompany don Marcos in the cultivation of the *milpa* in the plot he has cared for all his life. And Don Marcos is confused again: he does not know how and why after so many years of refusing to participate in the *milpa* and blaming him for such rejection his sons have suddenly decided to participate again when they have so many other things to do."

In closing the story, Esteva adds: "I have the feeling that Dona Refugio knows why."

The Sandovals have devoted a couple of generations (so far) to living into the meaning and significance of the modern Western notion of "development" and the intrusion of dubious assumptions that it entails. Development, they might now say, "raises us up" —which separates us from the Earth (below)— and thereby converts our lives of "conviviality" to lives of enslavement (to the goals "development" inculcates: material acquisition, alienation from Nature, fragmentation of community, etc.).

As Don Marco's children have peeled away the layers of "development," finding their way back to "autonomous" solutions of inspiration, reconnection, and discovery, they are creating a new version of community, one which can take judiciously from the offerings of the "developed" world the delimited benefits it might provide without destroying the integrity and coherence of their lives. Their journey is anchored by Dona Refugio, steadfastly remaining seated on the ground, in the center of the conversation, embodying the Feminine (Yin and Yang, we might surmise), and bringing it under and into her children.

Their experience might bring into sharp relief for us, as we near the end of this exploration of the social, economic, and political ramifications of Tantra, the question of whether, and to what extent, a strongly local and community-oriented life might be more conducive to the harmonious expression of *spanda* (that of each person as well as that of the group) than one that is highly individualistic, separated from nature and community, and fragmented by bombardment with commercial incitements to consumerism.

We might even find ourselves wondering, as we circle back repeatedly to such recurrent goals as relocalization, decentralization, honoring of *spanda* (creativity), and the elimination of violence, whether much of what we currently call "political" might simply shrivel up and disappear if the social issues pinpointed by Esteva and the economic ones targeted by Greco were effectively addressed on a wide scale. The "political" as presently conceived might be seen as an awkward attempt to control, minimize, or (at worst) harness the violence that runs through our institutions.

Emerging Revolutions III (A Rising Tide)

While the thoughtful, determined, and courageous peoples in small corners of the world like Oaxaca are creating examples of social, political, and economic systems that work, much is going on in the "developed" world itself. Countless individuals have lost interest in the competitive, consumption-driven stampede to the edge of the cliff, and have simply stopped. They are living like Jo and William, they are doing what feels right to them, what soothes and caresses Her – both the Her inside themselves and the Her that is Gaia – as well as the collective gathering power of Her energy that can be felt across the globe. For every Davos World Economic Forum [*] there is a burgeoning World Social Forum [**] that is lively and multifaceted, energized, and gaining in momentum each year—as the crowd at Davos looks progressively greyer, more dispirited and lost, and increasingly irrelevant.

There are also countless organizations, some one to two million globally by one count [***] – many of them not even funded by foundations – that go about their blazing of new trails with satisfaction and calmness, sensing that the path ahead is clear: In economic innovation alone, there are, an estimated 11,000 worker-owned companies in the United States—and more people involved in them than are members of unions in the private sector. And there are 120 million Americans who are members of co-operatives—a huge number, about a third of the population. [****]

---

[*]   An annual gathering of corporate, philanthropic, and political leaders who consider directions that global policy should take.
[**]   A much larger gathering than that at Davos, it draws thousands of community leaders, activists, and innovators to various venues around the world, mostly in "underdeveloped" countries.
[***] Paul Hawken, *Blessed Unrest, How the largest Social Movement in History is Restoring Peace, Justice and Beauty to the World*. New York: Penguin, 2007.
[****] Armoudian, Maria, "*The Economic Revolution Is Already Happening—It's Just Not on Wall St.*" AlterNet, October 7, 2009.

These pioneering groups apparently need no official endorsement, no validation, they seem attuned to their own *spanda*. There are more, spanning many fields of endeavor:

New food distribution systems are being established that parallel the commercial ones, but deal in local staples, grown sustainably, sought after by a newly aware clientele that wants to chew on a bite of something that has substance, deep flavor, and overtones of the history and traditions of the place they live. They are looking for a more rooted sense of satisfaction – an assurance that their food is nourishing on many levels: nourishing the community, the soil, and their souls, as well as their bodies.

There are local groups studying the herbs that grow around them and using them to heal themselves – despite the strained attempts of commercial medicine to paint such options as dangerous. There are people learning to make ethanol on a local level, install windmills, or do the wiring for photo-voltaics. There are geeks online risking prison to share software at no cost. There are countless young people who are "urban refugees," heading for the countryside and making themselves vulnerable in their utter lack of skills and know-how, but learning and discovering new delights and possibilities.

There are charter schools that teach with respect for each student's unfoldment as a unique individual, and, at the same time, cultivate among them the knowledge of how to function as a community of diverse beings.

And there are the activists who stand in the way of the bulldozers, who stop the delegates from entering the meetings of the WTO. They are skilled in non-heirarchical organization, and have no "leaders" who can be arrested. They pull delegates aside, give them paradigm changing information and then dissolve into the crowd, like the guerillas that they are. Their modus operandi is their message and they combat the established order by transcending it and functioning in the new way with which they wish to replace the old.

In thousands of different ways these people are walking away from the past and leaving it to crumble.

The tide is turning, and we are left to wonder: Will this satisfy Her, will it make Kali's rampage unnecessary? Or is *this*, itself, Her rampage? Is this Her quiet and sometimes not so quiet way of clearing the deck, of replacing the broken concrete – or building with it (urban permaculturists call it "urbanite," and use it to construct retaining walls for neighborhood terraces that grow vegetables, fruits, herbs).

Is it enough that a growing number of people are finding Her within – whether they think about it in those terms or not – and are acting *from* Her power? Is this new groundswell of empowerment enough to melt away the metal armor of the rigid, frightened, and twisted Masculine that has come to hold sway over the politics, the institutions, and the economics of the planet? Will the new consciousness happen in time? we want to ask...

Of course, we don't know. Perhaps, literally, it will not happen "in time." It may happen only as we move "*beyond* time, space, and causality," as Shiva describes the Third Eye reality. And what does *that* mean?! What will that *look* like? How on earth (or elsewhere!) do we manage such a mind-boggling possibility?

Again, we don't really know. But it seems clear that whatever that may be, we will be most likely to be able to meet the challenge if we are clear-headed, flexible, fearless, curious, and up for an "*uber* adventure."

To establish ourselves in that sort of state might turn out to be one of the most direct and accurate descriptions of the spiritual path that we will ever find. In the next and final chapter of this book, we will explore briefly what that *might* look like.

CHAPTER 5

Spirituality: from Violence to Pleasure

Where we return to the preeminence and primacy of Play
– the reducto ad absurdum of Western civilization –
and thence to uncover our longing for Kali.

F or westerners to talk about spirituality, there are two thorny issues that must be confronted: the ubiquity of fear and the trivialization of play. Fear is so pervasive that it obscures most inquiries.

We as a people are consumed with fear: We are sure we are being threatened; we are the target of malicious forces that are plotting our downfall or perhaps immediate attacks on our neighborhoods and cities. We have alarm systems in our homes, guns in our glove compartments, and multi-colored codes to advise us of exactly how terrified to be at any given moment. The level of fear that we manifest puzzles people from other parts of the world. Often they live with greater actual threats, but seem less consumed by fear.

At the same time (and not coincidentally, I hope to show), we are dismissive of play: It is something that is trivial – the pastime of children. It's what is done until you can get to the real stuff—the serious work of adults—making money, conquering empires (financial or other), acquiring social or political clout, becoming someone who *matters*. Childish things like play are set aside, at least until there is some reprieve with the arrival of grandchildren (when, if we are lucky, we get to play a little bit again....)

I believe that there is a deep connection between these two afflictions: endemic fear and contempt for play. I think that they are both rooted in our confusion about the nature of power. If power is, as our current languaging suggests, the ability to control, subdue – to crush the spontaneous creative offerings of others, the ability to get others to do our will, then, yes, there is little place for play there. In fact, in that case the world is a grim battleground, and we must always be vigilant, prepared to defend life and limb, to safeguard our very survival. (We might call it a "war mentality.")

One of my early teachers, John Stocks, a psychiatrist and innovative therapist, wrote persuasively about the incompatibility of preoccupation with survival and the ability to play. A child cannot play in the way that conduces to climbing the developmental ladder if she is consumed with uncertainty about her survival. Providing a safe container for her development (a home and family) or for her happy experiments (a playpen) is the precious gift that parents can offer.

And that exploration of her spontaneous actions, if protected and cultivated as we would protect and nurture a tiny seedling, will grow into a confident harnessing of her *spanda*, her *shakti*, her power. And if she continues to blossom in this fashion, she will emerge a powerful – and, at the same time, playful— woman. In other words, play is the trigger, the vehicle, and the basic *form* of true power. This is following our tantric definition of power: it is the capacity to create, to manifest, to birth something new and unique. In this tradition, in this world-view, in this enduring and subtly influential spiritual tradition, play and power are inextricable. And power is never a dark, abusive, force for disempowering others. We must use a different word for that, and probably the best one we have in the English language is *violence.*

But violence has so long been sold as "power" that we have accepted the equation. Where we have identified violence in the last four chapters, we could insert the word power, and it would feel right at home there to most of us. Those who buy off congress for their profit, we term "powerful." Where there is abuse, we talk of "power differentials." When the Earth is raped, we speak of "those in power" as responsible.

Not only have we equated power and violence, we have gone a step further: we have learned to think that the violence is not violence – it is simply the inevitable outcome of using power, that it is the only form power can take (even though, in fact, true power can never take that form).

And then, in another leap, we have come to reserve the word "violence" for a different – special—situation. It is "something others (evil ones) do." It is abhorrent, it has become by definition "other." No one we know does such things. Nor does any one who occupies a position of prestige in our society. If one of our leaders is accused of war crimes, that is preposterous. Only the unhinged would suggest such a thing.

This is played out in such graphic forms as the abuse at Abu Grahib prison in Iraq. In predictable fashion, we identified the "bad apples," the "others" who committed such atrocities, and demanded their punishment. We had little appetite for searching out the tacit (or the explicit) permission given the perpetrators, or tracing the policies and attitudes (that we might have supported ourselves) that made it all possible.

Confronted with further examples, with evidence that the problem is widespread—that the violence is systemic—we watch the horrors unfold on television and mutter, "We're good people, there's some other reason we did it. It wasn't *really* violence. It wasn't *torture*—let's clarify (read: *reshape*) the definition of torture."

Thus in our customary murky mixing up of power and violence, we fail to distinguish them clearly either intellectually or emotionally. So we end up *fearing* power because we have so thoroughly equated it with violence. If power is violent then in order to be humane and loving, I must renounce it. I must refuse to use my own power. To do otherwise I risk falling willy-nilly into committing some despicable act of catastrophic violence: irrevocable words, physical attack—who knows—even murder!

I must decline the promptings of *spanda* (there's no telling what it might lead to!) I must substitute some other cues to follow – rules of behavior, moral(istic) codes, the dictates of those whose status exceeds my own, or, that lacking, the consensus of popular opinion, even current trends, tastes or styles.

Instead of following my own creative inspiration, to start a company that sells healthy food, perhaps, I mistrust my instincts, my *spanda*, and discount such "silly ideas," and search instead for "a good job," often settling for work that directly or indirectly contributes to actions and trends in the world that I don't feel aligned with. [*]

Meanwhile, this inner ban on what feels right only reinforces my alienation from my authentic spontaneity, the already stringent prohibitions against accessing the Yang Feminine, which have grown out of the cultural roots we

---

[*]   The most accurate term for this sort of occupation is arguably slavery.

discussed earlier. Namely: misogynistic and homophobic aversions to acting from the Feminine—to acting from what is, in fact, *spanda*.

In this way fear of violence becomes fear of power, which is, in essence, fear of *spanda*, which is fear of the fundamental essence of life, the Life Force, and its most prototypical expression: creative play and our own playful living.

Fear of Transformation

And then, what's more, our fears work in the other direction, too: If Kali is powerful, and so "other" – then clearly She is violent, terrifying, terrible, probably terrorizing – maybe even a *terrorist*!

Of course, she is not "other." She is self. And She is not violent. She is *powerful*. [*]

A major obstacle to accepting that, to grasping the She that is an aspect of each of us – of me – is the inability to imagine that power can work: If everyone were living and acting from *spanda*, that would be chaos, wouldn't it? No. It would not. But if everyone is pretending to be moved by *spanda*, then, yes, the result is chaos and pandemonium.

But, if everyone were *authentically* spontaneous, there would emerge only actions that knit together harmoniously. (Whether we are able to perceive the harmony right off the bat, is another issue). All true *spanda* flows from the same Source and meshes seamlessly. This is merely a corollary of the holographic model of the universe: Each part is a manifestation of the whole.

That is the spiritual core that must (re) emerge if we are to lose our fear. Though we may be aware of a fear of chaos and destruction, beneath that is most often a fear of death and annihilation. Another way of saying this is that our (individual and collective) First Chakra is reverberating with survival issues.

Only when we can fully accept that we are a functioning part of something larger than us will we lose that fear—when we feel in our bones the truth of

---

[*]   See Appendix A: Who is Kali?

[**] Certain formulations of this recognition of oneness, encoded in and dependent on the Mythical (mythical in the Gebserian sense – see "Mythical Structure of Consciousness" in the Glossary and Gebser, Jean, in the Annotated Bibliography – i.e., partaking of the archetypal infrastructure of the group consciousness) elements of a given culture, might be termed *religious*. Another way of speaking of or communicating this recognition of oneness, framed in terms more universal, more accessible to people of diverse cultural backgrounds, might simply *spiritual*.

the statement that That is who we are, and when the detail of individual being is less important. This need not be a religious [**] belief, a question of dogma, or a matter of buying into a whole cultural world-view. It can be as simple as accepting the implications of current observations and understandings that bring holistic paradigms into evidence – such as the use of a holographic model for looking at how the phenomenal world around us functions.

Autonomy and Individuality

It's interesting to look at how this works in the Indic psyche where the precepts of Tantra were evolved and have been discreetly safeguarded for a thousand years. That structure of the psyche is "very unlike the atomistic individuality of western modernity," [*] which lays claim to the label "individual" by virtue of being isolated, separate, and disconnected. The Indic version of individuality, by contrast, has been described as having two distinct but complementary characteristics: First, it reflects the whole as does a part of a hologram does (thus it is termed a "holon"). Second, at the same time, it relates to a sort of hierarchical *center* of the whole (thus it is "mandalic," i.e., like the elements of a mandala relate to its center). [**]

In other words, the Indic version of individuality is not isolated. It is only functionally or operationally separate (sometimes and/or in some ways). And it is connected in two ways: to all parts of the whole (being a "blurry" representation of the whole); and in a more specific way to its Center. This Center of the whole is the continuously out-pouring origin of the whole (and, of course, of each of its parts). This is the unitary consciousness, which the practitioner of Tantra accesses through ritual and meditation.

The first of these characteristics, its nature as one fragment of the whole, includes a uniqueness, just as each part of the body may reflect general truths about who you are, but is different from the other parts—despite the fact that they all reveal the same totality. This is the same sort of relationship that we see between the parts of the body and the whole of it: awareness of this relationship shows up in "reading" the pulse, or the tongue, or the iris, or the face, or the palm, or the posture of the person, or the shape of the ear, or the behavior of his blood under the microscope. [***]

[*]   Prem Saran, Yoga, Bhoga, and Ardhanarishwara. See Annotated Bibliography.
[**]   See Saran: Indic individuality is both holonic and mandalic.
[***]   Each of these has developed into a sub-discipline in holistic medicine, roundly ridiculed by conventional medicine, and vulnerable to "debunking" because of the mentioned "blurriness" of the picture of the whole that it offers.

The nature of this holographic relationship between part and whole is most clearly illustrated by the hologram itself. A sort of "photograph," the hologram is produced by exposing the object whose image is to be captured to two laser beams that impinge on it from different angles. The interplay of the lasers is recorded on a plate in such a way that any fragment of the plate, when light is passed through it, will yield an image of the whole object (the smaller the fragment, the blurrier the image.) This is in contrast to conventional photography, where a fragment of the plate yields only a corresponding fragment of the image of the object. This technological feat was recognized as reflecting a fundamental property of the world, one ignored during the reign of linear, analytic consciousness. That property is the capacity of each part of a whole to reflect more than its own identity, but to reveal information about the whole as well.

This holographic model with the nature of the part as "holon," is now recognized as opening new frontiers in the study of life and the universe. It is a modern validation of the ancient belief that the microcosm reflects the macrocosm. The pulse is more than mere pulse: it reveals details about the nature of the entire body within which it is occurring. The cell is more than a mere worker drone, it contains information (e.g., in its DNA) about the whole organism. A small grouping of plants in a forest (a "guild" in permaculture jargon) is more than a group of randomly situated shrubs and trees; it reveals the principles of interrelatedness that reign all over planet Earth. We are more than simply "individuals" (in our commonly understood sense of that word); we are repositories of the wisdom of the ancients and the vision of the future. With our chakras and anatomical and physiological functions, we are exquisite miniature models of the universe!

This sets us up for an existence of serene freedom: We are fundamentally identified with the whole, and this is not something that can be taken away from us. We are it, it is us. In a certain significant sense, we need not fear for our survival.

And in addition to this holonic or holographic relation to the whole, there is also our specific and strategic connection to the Center of that whole.

That continuously outpouring Center, or *origin*, is the "spiritual" fulcrum around which existence revolves, and that, like the hub of a wheel, provides the quiet, calm vortex of what may look disconnected and random, but is, instead, "held" in orbit by that Center. That counterbalances the freedom that flows from our inalienable resonance with the whole. It is this simultaneous holding and freedom that makes authentic "play" possible. Spanda flows from the Center, and in doing so, continuously re asserts the Center's primacy.

Meanwhile, holonic resonance with the whole allows us to reinforce our contribution to the existence of the whole, even as we assert our uniqueness. In other words, attunement to Spanda and an ongoing life of Play, keep one aware of spirit, of spiritual connection. And, in turn, that awareness of the spiritual center supports and enables the exuberance, freedom, and fearlessness of play.

Hence is the spiritual a necessary foundation for play, for pleasure and for genuine *spanda*, and vice versa.

> *Embarrassed by Her formless Husband*
> *And Her own graceful form,*
> *She adorned Him with a universe*
> *Of myriad names and forms.*
>
> *In unity, there is little to behold;*
> *So She, the mother of abundance,*
> *Brought forth the world as play.*
>
> — Jnaneshvar

The great obstacle to this arrangement, and why it is mostly limited to the Indic psyche (or that of other Asians and indigenous peoples), is the typically western ego – which is the most dominant and characteristic feature of the Western psyche and constitutes its version of individuality. This ego tends to be stubbornly resistant to *spanda*, and clings to the habitual and to the intrapsychic status quo. In other words, it fears change – or at least true change, which would necessitate the "death of the ego" and the birth of a new one.

It tends instead toward preoccupation with the ego and its constituent habits, comparing, ranking, and polishing its facets, as one might a restored antique automobile or a collection of bric-a-brac. This personality, being glorified and shown in various competitions (as it were), is also ultimately subject, if it becomes the object of widespread adulation (a coveted goal) to being discredited and scorned. Therefore isolation, despair, and self-destruction become fetishized as a sort of alternative "ideal" of individuality – the starving, drug crazed artist, the romantic poet with his tubercular cough, standing on a cliff looking into the wind and contemplating suicide. The whole affair—the vaunted "individuality" of western societies—appears on close scrutiny, in the words of Indian anthropologist Prem Saran, "rather thin on the ground."

Indic individuality, on the other hand, which reaches its apotheosis on the tantric path, celebrates *spanda*, delights in play, and is fearless in the face of death. This is not meant as an inducement to the emulation of the psyche of the East by westerners. That's not possible, and would be undesirable even if it were. It has its own culturally determined mythical/archetypal structures that have, by and large, not been acculturated into westerners.

Rather what is intended here is to point out the current nature of individuality in the two settings and to open the possibility of a uniquely twenty first century, global *garden* of tantras – each of which devises its own characteristic way of remaining both holographically related to the whole and receptively connected to the unitary consciousness that can sustain it. To reach that goal will, it seems, require finding new ways to transcend the limitations of the ego and new paths to connection with Spirit so that the life of play can be enjoyed and the adventure of Tantra can continue its long history of morphing and reshaping itself.

A Note on the Writing of Kali Rising

Shiva and Shakti

They are like a stream of knowledge
From which a knower cannot drink
Unless he gives up himself

When such is the case
If I remain separate in order to honor them
It is only a pretended separation.

My homage is like that
Of a golden ornament
Worshipping gold.

— Jnaneshvar

A last bit on the application of Tantra

Tantra is about embodiment, diving into living the principles on multiple levels and allowing your body, energy, mind, emotions, and dream world to be danced, the steps choreographed by cosmically coordinated *spanda*.

We know we are living Tantra when we notice the interweaving of its principles and their application in the different facets of our lives: the outer relationships mirroring the inner, or tapas facilitating the creative eruptions of Her – *shakti/spanda*. We confirm the validity of the path as we trace these interactions from one sphere of activity to the other. So it has been that I see Tantra emerging in the writing of this book, even as it articulates the principles that bring it into being.

When I began to think about this book I only knew that I wanted to find a way to communicate the principles of Tantra as they had taken shape over the twenty years of my training. I spent years struggling to find a form, a format, for it.

Then I remembered the technique I had taught. If you: 1) apply Tapas to create a container (the Yin Masculine/Testicular); 2) nourish and care for yourself so that you are full and ready to overflow (the Yin Feminine/Nourishing Womb); 3) maintain your sense of curiosity and adventure (the Yang Masculine/Phallic); She, the one who is left (the Yang Feminine/Birthing Energy [*]) will show up!

Well...*when* She's ready, that is. So I learned to wait. *La guette au trou*, the French medical students on obstetric rotation used to call it: The wait at the hole – the arch – from which issues creation. When writing all the other books I had done, I worked hard, made an effort, spurred myself on. This time I lay down, put my feet up by the wood stove, and looked out the window at the budding trees, the birds, the flowering dogwood, the sun streaming in and then, as a cloud passes over it, ceasing for a moment, then lighting the room up again.... She's at play. She'll get to me.

And then She would: She would begin to speak, and I would jot down the lines, or get up, go to the keyboard, and type. The principle is sound: set up what you can: the Yin Feminine fullness and receptivity; the Yin Masculine structure or container – a certain quota of words a day; the Yang Masculine goal-directed determination, the desire to penetrate into the mysteries of the subject I am circling and poking at....

[*]   Or *shakti/spanda*

And await Her pleasure. And when She shows up, allow Her to move me, to be that deeply felt impulse to move, to create, to give voice to something greater than myself. What emerged was a conversation. I was a bit surprised, but intrigued. The voices were contemporary, and sounded like a teacher and a student.

Only after I had written down (and in places misunderstood or botched) a dozen pages of dialogue, did it occur to me who the parties were: He was Shiva, and She was Shakti. Of course! Why hadn't I thought of that? That is the classic format of a tantra! But the tone was not classic at all. Not only was the language very up to date, the dynamic between the two of them was quite contemporary. She was no longer the submissive feminine of the traditional *agamas*. On the contrary, she was a very active participant, in many ways the voice that steered the interchange in the direction it took. She was the Yang Feminine, in her most charming, witty, right-on-the-mark form. She stole the show.

And the result was, in fact, very much like the longed for dynamic between the inner He and the inner She. They have fun with each other, they are playful, yet their dance whisks us through the deepest and grandest questions of the cosmos – dropping hints about scores of others along the way—all in the most effortless manner imaginable.

And, in typical tantric fashion, this turned out to be the perfect format, since their dialogue serves as a model for the He/She meditation that is so central to the practice of this version of Tantra.

It is hoped that sharing this final piece of personal history will cinch the primary message of the book: that Tantra is fun, it is what happens when you quit forcing things to happen, it is liberating, it is more deeply and broadly spiritual than any earnest, well-meaning, moralistic effort can ever manage. It addresses core issues that are blocking the joyful unfoldment of a more mature and humane consciousness on the planet. It sweeps away sexism, misogyny, and homophobia, and undermines the foundation of the pervasive violence that could consume us. It even begins to dissolve away the fundamental fear of death that is our secret obsession.

I invite you to partake freely. I suggest you prepare yourself to let go your hesitation, your ego protection, and your fear of your own power. Let Shiva's dance be yours, and let Shakti run through your being and set it on fire. Whatever you think you have to lose, throw away. Celebrate the pulsing life of planet Earth.

The End!

APPENDIX

APPENDIX A

Who is Kali?
(And who is Shakti?)

Who is Kali? An archetype? A construct of our imagination? An artifact of archeological interest? An alien cultural symbol imported to justify feminist agendas? A dark object of adoration by tribal peoples in India's remotest outposts? A facet of Shakti?

She is all of these things and much more.

Kali is a figure with a long and multi-layered history. Although she has been worshipped throughout South Asia, She has traditionally been most popular in the outlying regions of India, its "corners," so to speak, away from the predominant mainstream culture: Kerala and much of the rest of the southern tip of the subcontinent, for example, or Bengal, Nepal and Assam in the extreme northeast, and Kashmir and neighboring areas in the far northwest.

While stories about Her, rituals dedicated to Her, and ways of depicting Her vary from one region to the other, She is generally seen as a goddess who both "encompasses and transcends" [*] the opposites of life. "She is, for example,

[*]   Jeffrey J Kripal and Rachel Felt McDermott, editors, Introduction to *Encountering Kali*.
[**]   Ibid.

simultaneously understood as a bloodthirsty demon-slayer, an inflictor and curer of diseases, a deity of ritual possession, and an all-loving, compassionate Mother." [*] Though in Bengal she may be pictured wearing fetuses as earrings, decapitating men—with a necklace of severed heads and a skirt of human arms—and living on the cremation grounds, her devotees still address her affectionately as "Ma" (Mother).

How do they hold all these contradictions? Here is a tribute to her by a contemporary Indian poet:

> *Is my black Mother Syama really black?*
> *People say Kali is black,*
> *but my heart doesn't agree.*
> *If She's black,*
> *how can She light up the world?*
> *Sometimes my Mother is white,*
> *sometimes yellow, blue, and red.*
> *I cannot fathom Her.*
> *My whole life has passed*
> *trying.*
> *She is Matter,*
> *then Spirit,*
> *then complete Void.*
>
> *It's easy to see*
> *how Kamalakanta*
> *thinking these things*
> *went crazy.*

> — Kamalakanta Bhattacarya

Just as there are many Kalis, there have been many reactions to her: Europeans were predictably scandalized and repulsed:

"No one can tell in what age it was that divinity revealed itself to the vision of some aboriginal or Dravidian seer in the grotesque form of Mother Kali, nor does any record exist regarding the audacious hand that first modeled...those awful features...crudely embodying in visible form the very dread of femininity always working in the minds of a most sensuous people, too prone to fall before the subtle powers of the weaker sex..." [**]

[*] Ibid.
[**] Hugh Urban, India's Darkest Heart, Kali in the Colonial Imagination in *Tantra: Sex, Secrecy, Politics, and Power in the Study of Religion.*

But scholars have catalogued [*] equally outraged reactions from Indians themselves, whether due to an internalization of the mores of their British and Mogul conquerors, or from a desire to "clean up" the image of their tradition and gain access to respect on the world stage, or simply their immersion in a mainstream culture that finds the perennial tantric counterculture abhorrent. In any case, Kali has been the object of scorn and cultural "purges," almost as often as She has been the object of adoration. The result is a constant ebb and flow of revisions and restorations of Her image and meaning.

For example in Orissa, on the East coast of India, where there is an active and longstanding Kali tradition, anthropologists interviewed 92 men and women in the neighborhood surrounding a twelfth century Shiva temple. They asked each what the popular calendar depiction of Kali – garlanded with skulls, holding a severed head and sword, with Her tongue out, and one foot on the supine figure of Siva—meant. What was the story it represented? 90 of them simply replied that that the protruding tongue reflected Her shame at standing on Her husband (an interpretation peculiar to that locale.)

The other two interviewees, both men close to seventy years of age and both former priests, gave more traditional tantric interpretations of the icon. E.g.: "She has her tongue out in anger; She is always angry, she is always creating and at the same time destroying life."

They had both participated in tantric rituals (worships, or *pujas*). "The goal," one of them explained, "is to acquire perfect knowledge and ultimate power. The naked devotee worships Mother on a dark, moonless night in a cremation ground .... Ordinary people cannot participate in such worship – if they were even to witness it, they would go mad."

These two (out of 92) viewed the image of Kali as a tantric goddess. All the rest saw in it only a moral lesson about the proper behavior of a wife. The researchers found that by examining scriptures dating back to the 15th century, they could trace the gradual evolution of Kali's story from that of a fearsome destroyer to that of an object lesson in family values in that region of India. Multiply that by thousands of communities over more than a thousand years, and you will grasp the overwhelming diversity of interpretations of Kali in South Asia.

In contrast to the story of Kali as upholder of family values – at the other end of a spectrum of interpretations of her—we find the Aghoris, particularly in the North of India, who live on the burning ghats (cremation grounds). These

[*] Cynthia Humes, Wrestling with Kali in *Encountering Kali*, pp 145-168.

Kali devotees are solitary ascetics, who deliberately embrace the status of "outcastes among outcastes" and yet serve by "literally 'eating the sins' of their mainstream...Hindu followers." The most famous are credited with "having the power, to not only swallow polluted and poisonous substances, but to transform them into harmless or benign residues." This they do by virtue of "their invocation of the Goddess, who by Her very material nature encompasses all substance. As the embodiment of all creation, She negates the very possibility of purity or pollution. Hence the Aghoris move far beyond standard Tantric ritual practice not only by invoking Her with the *pancamakara* – meat, fish, parched grain, wine, and sexual intercourse – but in addition by offering their feces and urine." [*]

At the other end of another spectrum, that of *contexts* for Kali worship, we find the Kali devotees of South India. There tantra was taught, not among wandering bands of saddhus or in solitary practitioners on the cremation grounds, as in the North, but within the intact structure of the extended family. In the south, it was often the women who convey this knowledge to the children and youths in their homes and who serve as the priestesses of the Kali temples.

Kerala

Spending a month recently in the states of Tamil Nadu and Kerala in the extreme south of India, I was deeply impressed by the confidence and authority that I sensed emanating from the women – so distinct from the attitudes of those in the north. The men, on the other hand, seemed more humble, self-contained, and unassuming than their counterparts up north. The presence of the goddess is palpable. In the North one might be greeted with "Jai Shiva," but in the part of Kerala I visited it was simply "Durga!" (a goddess closely related to, and sometimes overlapping with, Kali.)

Kerala is a repository of Kali traditions. Kali has been the central deity of the state for at least two thousand years. "Scholars concur in the opinion that Kali derives in part from the ancient Tamil deity Kottavai....Her blue skin (sometimes described as black) seems likely to describe the extremely dark skin hue of the residents of the mountainous regions between Kerala and Tamilnadu." [**]

---

[*] Gupta, Roxanne Kamayani, Kali Mayi, Myth and Reality in a Banaras Ghetto, in *Encountering Kali, op cit.*, citing an interview she did with Kala Baba, Vindhyachal, Spring Navaratri, 1990.
[**] Caldwell, p 253-5

South India was long thought to be the last stronghold of the dark-skinned Dravidian race, pushed there by invaders from the North. Though that view is now contested, [*] it does seem that peoples of Dravidian language groups have been the wellspring of much of the wisdom that indigenous traditions contributed to the shaping of Tantra.

Therefore, South India's notions of Kali should be of special interest to those trying to decipher Her deeper significance. The following autobiographical account [**] of Kali worship by a Tantra devotee who grew up in Kerala when the traditional extended family was still intact is intriguing. Note how the high prestige of women seems to dovetail with the importance of Kali:

"My village had many homes, principal among which were 108 priestly households of various sizes. These households, called *taravads*, were true matriarchies as opposed to the more common matrilineal systems prevailing in most villages in that part of the country. My childhood ... was ... joyful, living among an extended family of fifty-seven people, in a rambling three-hundred-year-old homestead."

"Matriarchs headed the households, governed the village through the Tantric Council and guided the agro-pastoral and religious affairs of our community. ... In our culture where every aspect of our way of life was taught by word of mouth and through direct apprenticeship, the role of the matriarch was indispensable. Time had distilled much wisdom into the matriarchs who served as reservoirs of cultural knowledge. The matriarchies of my village gave prime recognition to women in spiritual and temporal matters. This appreciation was most evident in spiritual issues, as women seers and tantrikas enjoyed superior standing compared to their male counterparts."

"The day-to-day life in our village revolved around the early morning-to-midnight worship performed at our main Kali temple. This temple rose from the center of the village, with the homesteads forming a crescent around it. ... We call the deity of our temple *Kula Bhadra Kali* ('benign Kali of the clans'), and She was central to our daily lives."

---

[*] The debate about the classic concept of Aryan/Dravidian conflict in ancient India has become highly politicized in the past few decades. Recent DNA analyses, however, suggest that there was a significant influx of East African ancestry into southwestern India as early as 50,000 years ago. (Satish Kumar, et al, (2008). The earliest settlers' antiquity and evolutionary history of Indian populations: evidence from M2 mtDNA lineage. *BMC Evolutionary Biology, 8* (1), 230.) If the arrival of European stock later is also confirmed, then some version of the classic interpretation may regain credibility.

[**] The account below is from the remarkable book byAmarananda Bhairavan, *Kali's Odiyya.*

Her devotees comprehended Kali in two distinct forms: the benign and the malevolent. The former was associated with Her creative and nurturing functions, and was the deity of the temple in the center of the village. [*] The latter form was associated with Kali's depredatory and destructive roles. She was relegated to a shrine in the forest.

That form of the goddess was known as "Kattu Kali (or Forest Kali) – also known as Raktha Kali, after the deep, crimson-black color" of her gory image. "In contrast to the benign image in the greater temple, this deity has a ghastly presence. Though She is the same divinity worshipped at the main temple, on the Night of Kali She assumed Her destructive functions. This manifestation of Kali was purposefully sequestered in this forest, away from all homesteads. In this gruesome form, Kali erupted one night each year, to devour the evil and the wicked among all life."

The women officiated in the temple all year round, except for this period. On this particular night, they were at home honoring the benign Kali and the ancestors with a sumptuous feast. Meanwhile, male priests were performing a ritual to awaken and honor the Forest Kali. They sacrificed a black male goat, and poured its blood over the Forest Kali. As soon as She was aroused from her slumber, She was offered human blood to set her on her rampage: "Kali devotees, immersed in divine rapture struck their own heads with scimitars. The blood that streamed forth was offered to this Kali." Under the sway of that extraordinary state of consciousness, they "recovered rapidly from their ghastly wounds."

The author considers this act a means of transporting "them into feeling they were one with the Universal Being, enabling them to go beyond body consciousness and ego attachments." We might imagine them in this way offering to Kali their own heads (egos) to add to those She wore as a garland around Her neck.

But even in Kerala things change. The author of the above account explains:

"The extended family I had experienced no longer exists. The matriarchies, extended households, and landed properties that sustained these homesteads have disintegrated under the impact of modernizing forces. The family shrines and ancient rituals performed there have disappeared with them. Imported cultures and lifestyles have pressured the younger generation to abandon old ways."

---

[*]   This would correspond to the Shakti of our dialogue in Part I.

During my own visit in early 2009, I saw the huge homes of extended families sitting empty. I asked my third generation Keralan Ayurvedic physician what had happened. "Many of the men are away working in the [Persian] gulf states. Those who are still here and many of the women are employed in IT." (That's "Information Technology" – the voices that answer most corporate numbers you dial in the West these days.) They live alone (as a couple, or apart, if one is abroad), too busy for the responsibilities of a large collective household—busy making the money necessary for the sleek automobiles parked by their new, smaller homes. They are, it seems, having their own fling with consumerism.

Sarah Caldwell, a Harvard cultural anthropologist, who has written extensively on Kali [*] sees this move away from the Mother centered society as beginning long ago:

"A historical shift...appears to have occurred over the past two thousand years in Kerala. Indigenous concepts of feminine power ([e.g.,] the Sanskrite *sakti*), once firmly lodged in female bodies and celebrated by women, were marshaled in sacred military rituals to enhance the multivalent, mysterious power of the king and the realm. Over time, as Sanskritic and Brahmanical [**] values predominated, women were marginalized from the rituals of power, while their embodied feminine potency was co-opted and imitated by male ritual specialists. [***] The essentially feminine character of the deity, with the concomitant values of sexual potential and violent rage still attached, became an attribute of men. [****] As Kali's worship came more under the control of Brahmanized elites, the earlier multivalent potency of the Goddess was reconfigured as danger, chaos, and pollution."

"Today, male ritual specialists dressed as the Goddess perform the rituals that once were the province of women.... The prior prominence of women [is] a role that is now almost entirely lost to women in Kerala as they attempt to raise their status by distancing themselves from everything connected to Bhadrakali."

[*]   See her book: *Oh, Terrifying Mother: Sexuality, Violence, and Worship of the Goddess Kali* and her film: *Ball of Fire: The Angry Goddess.*

[**]   This refers to the classical patriarchal order that is sometimes identified with Vedic culture. The Vedic has often played the role of the mainstream as against the countercultural role of the Tantric.

[***] This makes the above autobiographical account (from *Kali's Odiyya*) all the more remarkable. It lends credibility to that author's claim that his village was unique in being a "true matriarchy" rather than merely matrilineal, and suggests that his account is a rare glimpse into a sort of society that may have predominated thousands of years ago in Kerala, sporadically reemerging in isolated patches of the cultural soil still hospitable to it.

[****] Actually, compared to the distorted Masculine described in the body of this book, so alienated from its Feminine, this willingness to embody the transformative energy of the Yang Feminine, seems almost exemplary.

A scholar visiting her house in Kerala, Caldwell recounts, saw her pastiche of Kali images in the living room and said to her "in hushed tones, 'You know, nobody has Kali on their [altar] like that except black magicians [marginal religious figures who engage in harmful sorcery].'"

"Yet," Caldwell insists, "Kerala's Kali...was ever present, as a hidden potency....In every town and village, one could find Bhagavati [*] installed in a shrine; but her image was always enclosed in an inaccessible sanctum....In homes, the Goddess was hidden behind closed doors, dark and safe. Her mantras were inscribed on copper plates bound in secret closed capsules around babies' waists and necks. To place Kali at the center of life was not unusual, but to display her openly was...."

"Kali was always present as an unseen power that both enlivens and destroys....[She] is always moving, always present, always informing what is on the surface. Pressing those surfaces reveals her directly, in extreme and unusual moments like those created by ritual possession.

"Practices [such as] blood sacrifice, possession, self-mutilation, and ritual sexuality....features of Kali's worship have long been at the core of the religious practices and worldviews of aboriginal, Tantric, low-caste, and village traditions, particularly in the south and northeast of India. These non-elite traditions often center around conflictual models of divinity, immanent, embodied powers, and a deep concern with death and sexuality. Intense, engaged physical and emotional experience, rather than detachment and ordered ritual purification are their characteristic mode.

"To describe Kali as a goddess of 'outsiders' is to position ourselves as scholars alongside the elite Sanskrit texts that until very recently have been our main sources. We...miss the more interesting truths about Kali we can get by standing at the margins with the aboriginal, Dalit (literally 'oppressed,' the term favored by the people earlier called 'Untouchables'), Tantric, or female persons. The richness of such multiple views is well worth the effort and may radically alter our understanding of Kali." [**]

To fully understand Kali may mean being open to the collective truth of many views – even (or, perhaps, especially) when they are contradictory. Perhaps, it is the diffraction of Her through the lenses of many of us that reveals Her truth.

---

[*]   Bhadrakali, the terrible form of Kali.
[**] Sarah Caldwell, Margins at the Center: Tracing Kali through Time, Space, and Culture, in *Encountering Kali*.

Therefore, to the countless interpretations of Kali, I would like to add my own:

Kali is the personification, within the Mythical Structure of Consciousness, [*] of the awesome and often inscrutable power of the life force. She exists in the realm where such mythical figures or archetypes "live." As such She gathers and shapes the subtle energy underlying all phenomena and feeds it into the "ordinary world" – the particular reality of which we are most often conscious – shaping and impacting it as well.

The baffling contradictions between Kali's different facets, e.g., between her loving kindness and Her wild destructiveness, force us to let go our conventional way of thinking. It doesn't work. And only by letting it melt away can we "shift up" to a more encompassing perspective. In the language of the present book, we move toward the Integral Structure of Consciousness. From there we can grasp (albeit in a way that may be difficult or impossible to articulate) the deeper significance of the power that Kali personifies.

To attempt such an articulation we might say: She is both the matter-of-fact champion of transformation and the *power* that makes such transformation possible. At the same time, She is indifferent to the elaborate system of delusions that constitute human consciousness and that prop up our fragile sense of what is real and what is important. Because of this we cannot fathom Her rage and destruction – we simply cannot see that far beyond the familiar territory of our illusions. Her capacity for destruction (perhaps, more accurately, *destructuring*) goes beyond all we know and hold dear, therefore She is unimaginably terrible and overwhelmingly terrifying to us. She is the personification of what we most fear: the annihilation of our world and the obliteration of our sense of self, or ego. Nothing is safe from Her.

She embodies *shakti*, ultimate power – the only power there is: the power to create, to manifest. Once we grasp the enormity of Her power and the relentless way She uses it to clear away everything that blocks our transformation, our unfoldment, our Self Realization, then we will find ourselves naturally relaxing into Her embrace as does a child into the arms of its mother. After all, She knows – better than we do, better than we ever can!—what is for our ultimate welfare, what is the deepest reward of life, and She will insist that we move toward it, and will, in a fury, if necessary, rip away anything that distracts us and that stands in the path of that.

---

[*] See the body of this book or the glossary for the precise definition of this term. Mythical here does not mean "imaginary."

Having understood this, we need understand little more: I can rest at peace in her lap; She is Kali Ma, and I am her child. In this state I am able to receive my bit of the universal spanda, along with the quantum of shakti that accompanies it, and experience true power, both moving through me and focused—or refracted, as the case may be—by my own uniqueness.

She is the final dissolving of fear into love, for She is the force that we can "love to fear."

With this view of Kali in mind, we might re-imagine the unschooled widow, the tribal warrior, or the tantrika sitting on a corpse in the cremation grounds, gazing at the image of Kali Ma, absorbing the fact of a world She dominates, feeling – without the benefit (or handicap?) of intellectual training – his or her way into a deeper truth about the storm of life, the roll and pitch of heart breaking events. Finding a Mother who lives beyond fear and loves far beyond sentimentality or morality. Perhaps this is the enduring appeal of the terrifying face of Kali.

And Shakti? Who, then, is She?

While Kali is one form of the goddess, Shakti might be the prototypical goddess Herself. (At least in the view of the tantrika. Other Indic traditions may organize their cosmology differently). But *shakti* (lower case) also simply means power. From the Sanskirt root *shak-*, it literally means "to be able."

This significance of the word applies not specifically to the goddess who resides in the Mythical Structure of Consciousness, but instead reaches down into the Magic Structure, to designate the universal subtle life force. In this sense, *shakti* is the generic term for the power of that life force (the only power there is, though it exists and operates on more macrocosmic levels a well – i.e., beyond life on planet Earth). Abstractly, it can be related to other universals, e.g., *vayu*, the energy flow that results from the exertion of the power called *shakti*, and *karma*, a term which, in its most encompassing sense, indicates that which obstructs, or slows. The universal relationship between the three is represented as:

$$vayu = \frac{shakti}{karma}$$

where *vayu* is the movement of the specific material or immaterial phenomenon, *shakti* is the force applied, and *karma* is the resistance to that force.

To illustrate this universal relationship with concrete and familiar example of it:

$$\text{flow} = \frac{\text{pressure}}{\text{resistence}} \text{ or} \qquad \text{current (in amps)} = \frac{\text{voltage (in volts)}}{\text{resistance (in ohms)}}$$

Of course, there are other specific applications of this formula that operate on
non material levels. For example, psychologically, where the manifestation of
shakti is desire, the resistance might be habits, and the flow would be action to
fulfill the desire (even fulfilling a desire through fantasy – rather than actual
action—with habits of thought or defenses against ego-alien thought forms
operating to resist the desired imagination or fantasy.)

Shakti (upper case) as a name of the goddess, designates a figure, a primal
manifestation of that power meant by the first use of the word—that is to say,
She who participated in our dialogue of Part I. It is important to realize that
in the Indic mind these are not two separate "meanings" of the term, but flow
together seamlessly, power always bringing to mind the personification, the
image of the goddess always sensed as a the visible presence of power. The split
between the two that the western mind has constructed doesn't exist there. In
Gebserian terms the Mythical and the Magic have not been torn apart.

While on a cosmic level Shakti personifies the dynamic manifesting energy
that creates the universe, on a more limited level, the female consort of any
male person or deity might be referred to as "his shakti." To the extent that he
plays the Masculine role to her Feminine one she represents and manifests the
power they have access to as a couple. [*]

Shaktism is a term used to refer to the concentration of practice and devotion
primarily on Shakti (and only secondarily on Shiva). It regards the Goddess as
the supreme reality and all other deities male or female as merely diverse manifestations of Her. According to the Shaktisangama Tantra: "Woman is the
creator of the universe, the universe is her form; woman is the foundation of
the world, she is the true form of the body. In woman is the form of all things,
of all that lives and moves in the world. There is no jewel rarer than woman,
no condition superior to that of a woman." [**]

[*] Since, for example, Lakshmi is Vishnu's "shakti," Shiva's consort is sometimes conceived of as Parvati, rather than Shakti, in order, perhaps, to distinguish Her from the generic use of the term.
(Doing so, however, seems to result in Her becoming a bit more anthropomorphic and losing some
of Her flavor of universality.)
[**] Wikipedia

In the specifics of its philosophy and practice, Shaktism is very similar to Saivism. However, those who practice Shaktism, "focus most or all worship on Shakti as the dynamic feminine aspect of the Supreme Divine. Shiva, the masculine aspect of divinity, is considered *solely transcendent*, and Shiva's worship is generally relegated to an auxiliary role." [Ibid. emphasis mine.]

Our dialogue, because it gives Shakti more voice than do the more traditional tantras, might be seen as a "Shaktist" writing. Hopefully it would qualify as both Shaivist *and* Shaktist [*] – creating an inviting space for the inner marriage to be consummated.

[*]   The correct term here is Shakta

APPENDIX B

The Meditations and Tantra

W here are four meditations in this book. The main event is the She/ He Meditation that is offered between Parts I and II. This is the opportunity to bring into awareness your own internal version of the dynamic between Shiva and Shakti, between tapas and spanda—to launch your own adventure with Tantra.

Those experienced in meditation, those who have gradually learned to allow consciousness to shift into other "frequencies," or to enter "other realities," will probably find the meditation relatively easy to enter with little or no preliminary work.

For those new to the meditation process, Welcome! You are about to embark on a journey that could intrigue you for many years, perhaps the rest of your life.

To assist you, I have offered three additional, shorter preparatory meditations, which demonstrate the basic building block techniques that are the foundation of the longer She/He meditation. They are found at the end of each section of the dialogue. While meditation has long been a gradual learning, there is at this time a "readiness" on the group level—at the level of the "planetary mind"—to gain access to the process more easily, to ride the wave of multitudes who are experiencing subtle but powerful shifts in their consciousness. Because of that, you may, with the help of the three initial preparatory meditations, find yourself slipping into the She/He meditation with surprising ease.

Here is a brief orientation to the four meditations:

The first develops an awareness of the ascending and descending currents of subtle energy flow up and down the spine. This is basic to work with Tantra. Like a time-lapse photograph of traffic in a city at night, the more times you repeat this process with full attention, the more vivid are the main "streets" along which the vital energy or *prana* flows. This awareness is a foundation for further work.

The second is an introduction to the right and left major channels (*nadis*). It is an opportunity to experientially grasp the relationship of right and left sides of the body to Masculine and Feminine, and to the laterality of the breath.

The third Meditation on Breath deals with the union of right and left (*sushumna*). Here the invitation is to notice the difference between the lateralized (right or left) breath and its correlates on the one hand, and the unitary breath, where a sort of "observer," which can comprehend both comes into being.

These three steps prepare you to work with the inner dialogue between Feminine and Masculine, which brings the Shakti/Shiva dynamic to life within yourself.

APPENDIX C

The Book's Treatment of Gender

An apology is in order. The treatment of gender in this book is unwieldy and is often experienced as unnecessarily complicated. Unfortunately, I have been unable to find a way to talk about it successfully that is less so.

As mentioned in the introduction ("Orientation," as I have titled it) the terminology used here is that of the innovative Jungian analyst and Christian minister, Genia Pauli Haddon. Her ground-breaking work, *Uniting Sex, Self, and Spirit*, takes a giant step toward unraveling the confusion about gender that has plagued discussions of the subject in recent times.

What is particularly innovative is her use of anatomical and physiological referents to designate and reveal the nature of the various facets of gender expression (please refer to *Figure 3, Four Gender "Modes"* on page 47).

The "testicular" is the (yin) aspect of the Masculine, which has to do with *containment* – setting limits, providing structure that allows for relaxed and playful activity, without the anxiety and distraction of uncertainty. The testicle itself is a sort of living sculptural depiction of this function – it *contains* the genetic material of the male.

The "phallic" is the (yang) aspect of the Masculine, having to do with goal directed action, with the capacity to venture into with curiosity, to *penetrate*. What could more eloquently express this tendency than the erect penis?

Both feminine modes, active (yang) and passive (yin), are represented by the same organ, the uterus. This might seem to confuse the conceptual framework, not parallel in organization to the Masculine. In fact, it neatly suggests the variability of the Feminine, its phasic nature: first it is yin for a long time (pregnancy), then yang for a briefer time (birthing). The womb is again the prototypical manifestation of the receptive and nurturing characteristics of the Yin Feminine. Its "exertive" mode is equally perfect in its archetypal depiction of the Yang Feminine, the pushing out into manifestation of something both incomparably creative and supremely unique.

Haddon's book is also revealing in its treatment of the "bi-sexuality" of the human. She has no trouble attributing to women the capacity to access both their Feminine and their Masculine. But she does not mention such a capability for men. At the time she was writing, nearly 15 years ago, that was not inappropriate, since women were well ahead of men in their integration of what Jung called the "contrasexual."

Jung, however, considered *both* the woman's *animus* (her Masculine) and the man's anima (his Feminine) to be inaccessible to consciousness—to be only potentialities that manifested indirectly. Since his time (the late 1800's and early 1900's), that has changed. First women, and now, increasingly, men, are learning to bring consciously into play their contrasexual.

This has considerably broadened the behavioral repertoire available to both men and women. It has also, this book proposes, set the stage for the psycho-spiritual union of the Masculine and the Feminine – the "inner marriage" – which will activate the Sixth Chakra, (the Third Eye) and bring into play the Integral Structure of Consciousness toward which our planet is currently evolving.

While the schema mentioned is that of Haddon, the concept of the inner marriage as leading to opening of the Ajna (Sixth) Chakra is derived from Tantra, where it is implicit more than explicit. A further elaboration of Haddon's framework [*] is the distinction between the transformative and stabilizing axes. [**] While Tantra has a special focus on the intensity of transformation, it cannot sustain this unless the stabilizing, nurturing processes are brought

[*] For which I am indebted to Lorie Dechar, author of Five Spirits, and my co-teacher in many seminars.
[**] See *Figures 4* and *5* on pages 52 and 59

regularly into play. That is accomplished by an interaction of the Yin Feminine and the Yang Masculine (the "stereotypical" gender modes).

The Yin Feminine is the foundation of everything, because it relates to nurturance, replenishment, restoration, and juiciness. Without that, we dry up, burn out, and are incapable of rising to the intensity of birthing a new self. The Yin Feminine predominates for nine months, while birthing lasts but a day.

The Yang Masculine sustains life with directionality, purpose, and goals. While it has, in recent times, "got a bad rap" because it has been distorted to serve the violent aims of an impotent Masculine, in the context of a sane sense of purpose and goal direction, it is indispensable. These two principles, Yin Feminine and Yang Masculine, perform the classic dance of the hero and heroine, the romantic partners of fairy tales, the protagonists of the Hollywood love story. And their relationship matures into that of parents, partnering to provide protection, nourishment, guidance, and parenting of their fledglings. Their dynamic is fundamental to life. But without the spice of their transformative counterparts – the Yang Feminine and the Yin Masculine (that is, the Birthing Power and the Testicular containment) – their dance becomes bland and their romance stale.

Perhaps that is why the science of transformation is the soul of Tantra and why Tantra has the reputation of bringing excitement and fire back into relationships and sexuality. Without that, everything becomes humdrum or – even worse – moribund. In fact, disease is most often the expression of thwarted transformation – and healing the *reactivation* of the transformative process.

Mental, Mythical, Magic

Jean Gebser's Structures of Consciousness
And the Mandukyopanishad

Eastern spiritual traditions, the more ancient Western spiritual traditions, many indigenous cultures and traditions, the older learned traditions of countries such as China, Japan, and India – in fact pretty much everyone except the European oriented societies of the last five to seven centuries – assume that human life and consciousness extends through various dimensions (what we will call here "realities"). In other words, that the "ordinary" consciousness which so fully preoccupies us in our modern (urban or urbanized) civilization, is only part (even a relatively small part) of our "home," our "space," our "birthright."

While this fact has been ignored (maybe "banished," is a better term), for a long time for most of us, it continues to reappear, both from the attempts to forge a global community (not everyone willingly buys into the more limited sense of what constitutes human life that the economic giants assume), and from the spiritual seeking that wants to mine all the great traditions for much needed wisdom and guidance.

Though the academy (and the extensions of their viewpoints out into the workaday world), has, on the whole, maintained a resolute resistance to such "unscientific" [*] notions, it is beginning to wear away a bit around the edges. A prime example of what is pushing through such fraying resistance is the work of Jean Gebser (see Annotated Bibliography), who collated the plethora of learned writings of the mid-twentieth century so as to demonstrate the (re) emergence of the spiritual. He also detailed the rich multileveled texture of human consciousness. His work is summarized (simplistically) in the outline below, has begun to have significant impacts on current thinkers.

Meanwhile, in the traditions that surround and support Tantra, we find parallel formulations dating back over a thousand years. The most notable is the Mandukyopanishad (the most succinct of the Upanishads, amounting to a mere 12 verses), which corresponds with astounding precision to what Gebser came up with from his (almost exclusively) European sources.

The summary outline below is offered as a rough synthesis of Gebser and the Upanishad, in order to orient the reader to the context of Tantra: the multilayered composite of what Gebser called "Structures of Consciousness."

Realms of Consciousness: the "realities" within which Tantra is explored*

Waking Consciousness (*Vishva*)
Everyday "Ordinary" Conciousness. Similar to Gebser's Mental Structure of Consciousness. Classic Greece and post Rennaissance Europe. Linear time, three dimensional space, causality. Ego. Duality. "Perspectival," Triangular. Intellect. Sex as physiologic; as taking ownership of, as commodity.

Dream/Dreamlike State (*Taijasa*)
Archetypes, The story. Similar to Gebser's Mythical Structure of Consciousness. Medieval—age of troubadour, epics. Cyclical time (not linear), two dimensional. Causality weak/questionable. Group consciousness more than individual ego. Polarity. Circularity. Imagination. Sex as ritual, as primal drama.

Dreamless Sleep/"Trance" (*Prajna*)
Awareness of energy. Similar to Gebser's Magic Structure of Consciousness. Rhythm, drumming. Tribal consciousness. Timeless, Spaceless. No causality in conventional sense (allowing, not causing). Merger of group consciousness with nature. Unity with the natural world. Magic. Sex as energy exchange/flow.

[*] For those who wish more empirical data to back up this notion of Structures of Consciousness, see Anna Wise's book in the Annotated Bibliography.

Integral (*Turiya*)
Emerging consciousness on planet now – overlay of above three "transparently." Gebser's Integral Structure of Consciousness. Holographic consciousness. Time, space, causality not constraints. "Cosmic" consciousness, "Enlightenment." Sex as physical/archetypal/energetic/spiritual altogether.

* * *

SOURCES:
Jean Gebser, *The Ever Present Origin*
The Mandukyopanishad

*The order here is that of the Mandukyopanishad (as are the italicized terms). These "realms" of consciousness are listed in the order in which they are encountered during the meditation process: one starts with the "ordinary consciousness" and drops "back"—or "down" (or "up"!)—to the more subtle and less obvious Structures (Gebser's term). Gebser himself, on the other hand generally arranges the Structures "epigenetically," that is to say, according to how they seem to have originated in the course of human history. (Incidentally, this is problematic, as Gebser confesses, since his work, and the Upanishad as well, throw a shadow of doubt on the ultimate truth of linear time perspectives of this sort.)

APPENDIX E

Adaptations of Traditional Tantra In *Kali Rising*

The modifications made by this book in traditional tantra to adapt it to a western audience are discussed in the introductory pages, "*Orientation*," page 1. There are other tenets already implicit in the tradition that have been made more explicit, and in some cases extended:

1) The epigenetic schema, absent from mainstream western thought, but crucial to tantra's view of human evolution – i.e., moving into the 3rd eye consciousness (beyond time, space, and causality). My teacher did speak of this in broad terms, but there is no general agreement in tantra as to how to deal with this concept—i.e., the possibility of a mass, planetary shift as opposed to simply the emergence of the sixth Chakra consciousness within individual sadhakas.

2) The dynamic between *tapas* and *spanda*: The consideration of tapas and spanda as a sort of dynamic dyad, is as far as I can tell, an innovation that departs from the traditional Indic treatment of these two subjects. I have felt justified in taking this liberty because they do seem to have opposing/complementary tendencies that become apparent during the practice of Tantra. If that is true, why would they not have been considered before in this "interac-

tive" manner? My best guess is that it has to do with historical and cultural factors: each of the two terms is the focus of a quite distinct school of thought, so that they were not likely to be encountered together. Second, *tapas*, as is noted in the text of this book, is not discussed in much detail anywhere, since it seems to be such a cultural constant and of such universal importance in the Indic world that it needs little comment.

3) The difference between Yin and Yang Masculine and Feminine: Clearly such a reductionistic distinction would be unlikely in the tradition of Tantra. Its utility lies in its accessibility for the western student. The various schools of Tantra commonly acknowledge the various manifestations of the goddess – some more about transformation – birth and destruction – others more nurturing and "benign." But they merge and blend in myriad ways that, while familiar and undisturbing to the Indic consciousness, can be disorienting for the Westerner.

4) Dialogue between Masculine and Feminine: Swami Rama taught the use of the Inner Dialogue as a general practice; the focus of this technique on the integration of Masculine and Feminine specifically has arisen from the emphasis on the Inner Marriage.

5) "Everything is an experiment." Though this is clearly implicit in classic tantra, its emphasis as a general principle is again drawn from the teachings of Swami Rama.

6) Pleasure and play are at the center of Tantra as a spiritual path: this is another insight implicit in Tantra whose emphasis in this book is due to the extent to which it is absent from the Western world view.

All this, I hope, will serve to render what is offered here more relevant to the needs and challenges of the current westerner – and perhaps to the needs of those global citizens steeped in western culture, as well. For what I am struggling to present is a view of our current planetary challenges as seen through the lens of Tantra, and of the solutions that present themselves when those challenges are viewed from such a tantric perspective.

GLOSSARY

Many of these terms have more than one definition. In those cases, the span of meanings is represented.

A

Alchemy: Medieval science of transmutation. Alchemy historically gave rise to chemistry, which further studied the physical processes carried out in the Alchemist's retort (now the test tube), but dropped the study of the subtle changes occurring in parallel in the inner world of the person doing the experiment. The most prominent schools of Alchemy were the Egyptian (and by extension, European), Chinese, and Indic (more specifically tantric).

Archetype: A term popularized by Carl Jung to indicate primal figures in the psyche that have organizing functions and emotional charge. A component of the Mythical. A modern psychological term used to denote gods and goddesses.

Ardhanarishvara: The "half and half god." An icon representing both Shiva and Shakti; representing the god on the right and the goddess on the left, so that the left side has feminine, and the right masculine features, thought to indicate that the human is both masculine and feminine.

C

Chakra: Wheel. A whirling energy center that is thought of as the coordinating point between various levels of function: physical, subtle energetic, and mental. Seven major chakras are those commonly mentioned: Root (anal), genital or Sacral, Solar Plexus, Heart, Throat, Third Eye, and Crown.

F

Feminine: Typical of the female, though not limited to those with a female body. The "feminine principle" has a much broader significance: it is the aspect of the phenomenal world whose nature is most clearly represented by the function of the uterus, but it is not limited to female-bodied humans or even to "ordinary reality," manifesting in the Mythical Structure of Consciousness, as well as, to a lesser extent, in the Magic Structure also.

G

Gaia: The Earth. The recent re conceptualization of Earth as a single living entity, referred to as feminine.

Ganesha: The son of Parvati. The elephant-headed god. Though he is sometimes considered to be the son of Shiva as well, according to some of the classic stories, he was fathered by Surya, the god of the Sun in response to the entreaties of Parvati. He represents domestic harmony, and is often thought of as the prototypical mediator.

Gebser: Jean Gebser (1905-1973) was a European philosopher and professor of consciousness studies. He correlated vast expanses of information and concepts from the emerging fields of knowledge in the first half of the twentieth century in the West, and developed the first extensive and sophisticated approach to the study of consciousness as a central human phenomenon in the European influenced world. His work was distinguished from other academic efforts in this direction by its comprehensiveness and its insistence that coming developments in consciousness would involve a reemergence of the Spiritual.

H

Hologram/ Holographic: The hologram is a form of capturing an image on a plate through the use of laser beams. Its most intriguing characteristic is that all its content is contained in any finite part of itself (though at a lower resolution). In other words you can know the whole by examining any piece (though with less clarity and detail than you get by looking at the whole thing). An awareness of this technological advancement triggered new notions about the nature of the phenomenal universe. Physicist David Bohm suggested that all forms are holograms embedded in a universal hologram. The thinking that emerged from this discussion in western scientific circles moved considerably closer to that traditional in the East. In this book, the holographic model or paradigm is offered as a way of grasping the holonic aspects of Indic individuality (see Prem Saran, *Yoga, Bhoga, and Ardhanarishwara* and *The Holographic Universe*).

I

Ida: One of the two primary nadis (subtle energy channels in the human). It runs from the First or Root Chakra up alongside the spine to the left nostril, activating the left side of the body and the right side of the brain. Ends at the Third Eye (the point between the eyebrows). Breathing through the left nostril activates this nadi.

Indic: Of the culture and traditions of historical or present-day India. May apply to peoples and trends that are not of the current geopolitical entity we now call India, e.g., Nepal's attitudes towards and practices of Tantra.

Indra: Often termed the "King of the Gods;" his status varies from one of the multiplicity of spiritual traditions in India to the next.

Inner marriage: The union of the masculine and feminine aspects of a person within that person – as distinguished from the union of two persons in the outer world.

Integral Consciousness: See also Turiya, the Integral. A state of consciousness that does not divvy up human consciousness into serially held sectors. Up until now, this latter has been the dominant mode, and in the course of a twenty four hour day one customarily visits sequentially 1) the everyday waking consciousness, 2) the dream world, 3) the realm of dreamless sleep, and 4) a sort of union with Oneness. Integral consciousness is considered a further step in the development or evolution of human awareness that involves integration of what was before kept separate for lack of the ability to hold them together. Gebser describes this holding together as transparency.

J

Jnaneshvar: (Gyan-esh-war) Was a thirteenth century Indian mystic poet. Born in 1271 (therefore roughly a contemporary of Meister Eckhart in Europe and Rumi in the middle East), he completed his life work and left an indelible mark on the spiritual traditions of his homeland by the age of 25, at which time he voluntarily left his body. His poetry and prose writings, done in Marathi, were among the first to establish it as a literary and learned language.

K

Kali: Feminine of Kala, time. A major aspect of the goddess. A goddess who wreaks destruction on everything standing in the way of transformative change. She is represented and perceived in a variety of ways, most often with a garland of skulls or severed human heads around her neck and a skirt of severed arms around her waist. Her tongue is dripping with blood and she holds instruments of destruction in her hands. Other versions include a benignly, nurturing, and maternal image (though such a conception of Her will often also include an alternate guise that is more severe).

Kundalini: A serpent-like ascending stream of energy that emerges from the region of the pelvis to activate, re-organize and transform the energy centers (chakras) situated along the spinal cord above. This reconfiguration of chakras is the subtle energy facet of the overall transformative process often referred to as "self-realization" or "enlightenment."

L

Lingam: The phallus. A sculpture or monument that is upright and intended to represent Shiva. Some lingas may be carved and or painted to be realistic depictions of the penis. Others are more abstract geometrical forms.

Ludic: That which has the characteristics of play. (A term rarely seen, but favored by Prem Saran, Indian anthropologist and writer on and practitioner of Tantra, and whose work is referred to a number of times in this book.)

M

Magic (as in the Magic Structure of Consciousness): Term used by the European philosopher Jean Gebser to designate the structure of consciousness (also his term) that supports or is the field for events that primarily involve subtle energy, light, and non-imagery. It is neither verbal nor easily described verbally. Gebser's "Magic" closely corresponds to the Upanishadic term *prajna*, often translated into English as "first knowledge," i.e., awareness of the first step or stage of manifestation. This field or "reality" is considered to exist in a closer relation to the source of all phenomena than the fields of the Mythical or the Mental (and to "seed" or give rise to them).

Male chauvinism: Attitude or behavior which assumes and asserts (even if unconsciously) that men are superior to women and rightly hold a position of authority over them.

Masculine: Typical of the male, though not limited to those with a male body. The "masculine principle" has a much broader significance: it is that aspect of the phenomenal world whose nature is most clearly represented by the anatomy of the male genitals, but not limited to male-bodied humans or even to "ordinary reality," manifesting in the Mythical Structure of Consciousness, as well as, to a lesser extent, in the Magic Structure also.

Mental (as in the Mental Structure of Consciousness): Term used by the European philosopher Jean Gebser to designate the structure of consciousness (also his term) that constitutes our "everyday waking consciousness." This closely corresponds to the Upanishadic term *vishva*. Both Gebser and the Upanishads call into question the assumption that the "reality" of ordinary consciousness is more "real" than that of other structures of consciousness.

Mythical (as in the Mythical Structure of Consciousness): Term used by the European philosopher Jean Gebser to designate the structure of consciousness (also his term) that supports or is the field for dream imagery, archetypes, and other elements that serve as the infrastructure of the psyche. Gebser's "Mythical" closely corresponds to the Upanishadic term *taijasa*, often translated into English as "the dream world." Both Gebser's use and the Indic are to be distinguished from the "dream world" of common parlance in the West, since unlike it, they both assume that this consciousness is "prior to" or "the source of" our ordinary waking world – rather than a product of it.

N

Nadi: River; a channel through which subtle energy moves. The major two nadis lie along either side of the spine and are called Ida (on the left) and Pingala (on the right). The central channel, which opens with the left (the Feminine) and the right (the Masculine) reach union is called Sushumna. (See also Inner Marriage.)

O

Outer marriage: The union of two persons in the outer world as distinguished from the union of the masculine and feminine principles within a person.

P

Parvati: The consort of Shiva. She is considered to be one of the forms of Shakti. Shakti is also the term for potential energy and for power, whereas the figure of Parvati is surrounded by more human-like stories about her, her family, and her history.

Permaculture: The conscious design and maintenance of productive ecosystems to support diversity, stability and resilience. Includes agriculture, forest management, the human culture of community, and application of its principles in inner personal evolution; A system for practical worship of the feminine (as Gaia); A collection of indigenous practices for harmonious, embodied, and spiritually fulfilling living.

Phallic: That which has the characteristics of the Yang Masculine: adventurousness, goal directedness, penetrating; The capacity for penetrating insight; Also referred to as the Yang Masculine.

Pineal gland: The intercranial gland that secretes melatonin, is light-sensitive and is associated with the Sixth or Ajna Chakra.

Pingala: One of the two primary nadis. Running from the First or Root Chakra up alongside the spine to the right nostril, and activating the right side of the body and the left side of the brain. Ends at the Third Eye (the point between the eyebrows). Breathing through the right nostril activates this *nadi*.

Power: As used in this book the term signifies the creative potential, or the ability to manifest or birth something genuinely new. A capacity of the Yang

Feminine. The essential nature of *shakti*. Power, as defined in this book, and usually in the tantric teachings, is exclusively an aspect of the Feminine. There is, in Tantra, no such thing as "masculine power."

Prajna: The Sanskrit term used in the Upanishads (e.g., the Mandukyopanishad) to indicate deep, dreamless sleep. It is considered to be an immersion in a relatively undifferentiated consciousness and a regularly recurring reunion with the unitary consciousness from which individual consciousness arises.

Prana: Subtle energy. *Prana* in Indic sciences is the subtle energy that circulates in pathways called *nadis* through humans and animals.

R

Reductionism: The post renaissance trend toward reducing every phenomenon to its parts and attempting to infer its nature from that of those separate parts.

Retort: The container within which the alchemist combines his reagents so that they will interact. Their interaction was triggered as the result of a synergy between it and the dynamic transformative process going in within the alchemist himself. They were mutually catalytic to one another. In tantric work the relationship with another person may serve as the retort, and resonate with the inner relationship within the individual between his own Masculine and Feminine.

S

Shakti: Energy, power, creative force. The complement of the light of consciousness. Also, (in upper case here) Shakti is the goddess who is the consort of the god Shiva.

Shiva: A Indic god who represents the merging of austerities (*tapas*) and wild erotic enjoyment (*bhoga*). Shiva in some Indic traditions is considered the chief of all the gods, in others he is subordinate to Indra or Brahma, or Vishnu. He is highly revered by the tantric cults and traditions, and in fact, the formal philosophical articulation of Tantra is often termed Shaivism ("of Shiva").

Sixth Chakra: the energy center that lies superficially near the surface of the forehead between the eyebrows. The deeper center that lies behind the point between the eyebrows in the region of the center of the skull and at or near the pineal gland. Also termed, in Sanskrit, the Ajna Chakra, meaning "a little knowledge" (activation of the Seventh Chakra bringing a vaster "knowing").

Spanda: The primordial throb which gives rise to life. Related to the English word "spontaneous." That which leads to action that is of a deeply "authentic" nature.

Structure of Consciousness: A term favored by Jean Gebser, European philosopher and writer on consciousness. The structures of consciousness are specific fields that are suited to the awareness of and experience of their respective preoccupations: the Mental, the Mythical, the Magic, and the Archaic (connection with Oneness or Source). He posits the emergence of a new structure, which he calls the Integral, beginning in the last half of the twentieth century.

Sushumna: The central *nadi*. The breath when it is flowing equally through the two nostrils. The activation or "opening" of Sushumna is considered necessary for the Sixth Chakra to be fully activated. It is a tantric teaching that this physiological shift is dependent on the psychological integration of Masculine and Feminine.

Svadisthana: the Sanskrit term for the Second or Genital Chakra, which lies at or near the sacrum. Literal meaning: "Her own home," or "Her true home." Taijasa: The Sanskrit term used in the Upanishads (e.g., the Mandukyopanishad) to indicate the realm of consciousness where dream images are found and where organizing and emotionally charged archetypal figures operate.

T

Tantra: A scripture, often in the form of a dialogue between Shiva and his consort. A school of thought and spiritual practices designed to attain unity with the Absolute.

Tapas: A practice central to Tantra that involves the conscious, selective, carefully delimited, and voluntary declining to act on (and thus perpetuate) a habit (a physical or mental action that has become automatic and repetitive).

Testicular: The characteristics of the Masculine that allow for containment and protection. This includes "husbanding," patience, steadfastness, forbearance. The capacity to perform *tapas*. Also called the Yin Masculine.

Turiya: The "Fourth State." In the Vedantic (Upanishadic) writings, this is the term used to indicate the composite of the everyday waking consciousness (*vishva*), the dream world (*taijasa*), and the world of dreamless sleep (*prajna*). Turiya occurs when the other three are held "transparently" (i.e., as one would view a series of transparencies prepared for projection that have been laid in a pile over a light and viewed together).

V

Violence: As used in this book the word is defined as the crushing or destruction of another person's creativity, an abrogation of their power. Usually understood here as a substitute for accessing ones own power and creativity. Often a result of resistance to or fear of ones own Yang Feminine.

Y

Yang Feminine: The aspect of the Feminine (in either a woman or a man) that involves pushing-out-into-manifestation and birthing (as opposed to the receptivity and nurturing nature of the Yin Feminine). *Shakti*, power. The exertive womb.

Yang Masculine: The phallic. The aspect of the Masculine (in either a woman or a man), that is adventurous, goal-oriented, targeting, and involves penetrating actions (as distinguished from the steadfastness, patience, and *tapas* of the Yin Masculine).

Yang: A term from the Taoist tradition (a first cousin to yoga and Tantra). It denotes that which is (relative to something else) more active, light, warm, and assertive. In this book it is used (*a la* Haddon) as a way of distinguishing the more assertive aspects of Masculine and Feminine from those that are less active and assertive.

Yin Feminine: The aspect of the Feminine (in men as well as women) that involves receptivity and nurturance (as distinguished from the pushing-out-into-manifestation, birthing nature of the Yang Feminine). The gestative womb.

Yin Masculine: The testicular. The aspect of the Masculine (in women as well as men), that is steady, resourceful, containing (*tapas*), and "husbanding" (as compared to the goal-oriented, penetrating nature of the Yang Masculine).

Yin: A term from the Taoist tradition (a first cousin to yoga and Tantra). It denotes that which is (relative to something else) more receptive, dark, cool, and passive. In this book it is used (*a la* Haddon) as a way of distinguishing the less assertive aspects of Masculine and Feminine from those that are more active and assertive.

Yoni: The vagina. Often the base into which the lingam is mounted. The yoni is also sometimes related to the arch and the term Archaic, when that is used (e.g., by Gebser) to represent the Origin of all things-- the Source, or *Ursprung*.

ANNOTATED BIBLIOGRAPHY

A guide to the further study of Tantra

Abhayananda, Sri Satguru, *Jnaneshvar: The Life and Works of The Celebrated Thirteenth Century Indian Mystic-Poet.* See glossary entry on Jnaneshvar.

Ballentine, Rudolph, MD, *Radical Healing, Integrating the World's Great Therapeutic Traditions to Create a New Transformative Medicine.* This book on holistic medicine is woven around the principles of Tantra, though that is mentioned little in the text. It is designed to be pre eminently a handbook for self-help, though it is intended to supply the rationale and theory necessary to satisfy the professional or well-read layman. The center section, titled Foundation Stones, details the basic principles of nutrition, detox, and exercise that are fundamental to creating a state of health that will support intense tantric practice. (In the back of the book is also a Self Help Index that gives specific suggestions for use of the natural medicine modalities described in the body of the book to address common ailments and conditions.)

Boyd, Doug, *Swami.* Doug, with whom I traveled in India in the 70's, was the son of Alice Green, wife of Elmer Green, one of the pioneer developers of biofeedback at the Menninger Foundation, in Topeka, Kansas, where Swami Rama, my teacher, came in the sixties to be research consultant and subject. It

224 ANNOTATED BIBLIOGRAPHY

fell to Doug, a young man at the time, to be a sort of secretary and helper to the Indian swami. His tales of the experience, the culture clashes, the comic incongruities (e.g., Swami Rama repeatedly picking up the receiver and yelling, "Hello, hello....." to no response, until Doug explained that when a call is coming in one must wait for the phone to ring.) I recommend this book because, to some extent, getting to know Swami Rama is tantamount to getting to know Tantra (at least the Tantra I am endeavoring to represent).

Dyczkowski, Mark. *The Doctrine of Vibration, an Analysis of the Doctrines and Practices of Kashmir Shaivism.* Kashmir Shaivism, a philosophical system whose cornerstone is Abhinava Gupta's *Tantra Loka*, written over a thousand years ago, is generally considered to be the most sophisticated philosophical interpretation of tantra. This book, by one of the foremost exponents of that tradition, focuses on *spanda* as discussed in that tradition, and is a scholarly and nuanced interpretation of the *Stanzas of Vibration (Spandakarika).* Especially relevant is Chapter 4, titled "Shiva and Shakti."

Esteva, Gustavo, and **Prakash**, Madhu, *Grassroots Post-Modernism, Remaking the Soil of Cultures.* A fascinating re-visioning of culture in the light of indigenous traditions – those of both East and West. Esteva, a protégé of Ivan Illych, is one of Latin America's most brilliant and original thinkers. His co-author (and, at the time of writing, wife) did her PhD in education in New Delhi, and is currently a professor at Penn State. Together they "dig deep into their own encounters with what they call the 'social majorities' of their native Mexico and India, [where] they see ... evidence of a will to live in their own worlds according to their own lights." (From the end sheet comments – *Kali Rising* would term that *spanda* or the Yang Feminine.) Here (and elsewhere) Esteva calls this "autonomy," and offers the example of Zapoteca culture in Oaxaca (his grandmother was Zapoteca), as an example of how this can be made the basis of a local, community based political system in today's world. Esteva has also been closely involved with the Zapatista revolution in neighboring Chiapas, and writes lucidly about the significance of that stand against global corporatism.

Gebser, Jean, *The Ever Present Origin.* This book, for the reader who loves books that are challenging and offer huge rewards to patient and careful study, has marked a sea change in Western thought. Gebser painstakingly gathers the many strands of evidence of a paradigm shift that began in the early twentieth century in Europe and the West, to support his claim that we were (in the mid century) at the beginning of what he calls a "mutation" of consciousness that would both lift us out of the limitations of time, space and causality and bring us back to connection (of a more thoroughgoing sort) with the Spiritual. The volume as published currently was originally two (lengthy!) books, the first laying the profoundly erudite and solid foundation, and the latter comprising a survey of the major fields of his day, revealing how each was being reshaped by the emerging mutation. Gebser's work has been immensely influential in a number of fields, where respected thinkers owe him a major debt of gratitude.

Greco, Thomas H., Jr, *The End of Money and the Future of Civilization.* A surprisingly intelligible book on money and finance and how its current official version hobbles us with ever growing debt. Greco has become something of an authority on alternative systems of exchange and elucidates their advantages in clear and concise terms. Our monetary system is one of the chains that traps us in fear, disempowerment, and enslavement. Creativity (spanda) will be unleashed more readily with a revision of our system of credit. Greco describes a local, community-based *credit clearing system*, which is easily implemented, allowing us to step free of the tentacles of the current financial behemoth.

Haddon, Genia Pauli, *Uniting Sex, Self, and Spirit.* This book was of great value in putting together the current work. Haddon, whose book was self-published has not so far reached the large public with it that it deserves. The opening pages of the book, however, are filled with laudatory comments from the who's who of cutting edge thinkers on gender. She has been called a second generation feminist. What is brilliant about this book is Haddon's return to the basic facts of anatomy – not to tie us to biologically bound conventional gender roles, but to liberate us from them. She uses the concise eloquence of the form (primarily of the genitals) to decipher the function. Hence the distinction between the yin (testicular) Masculine and the yang (phallic). This offers a way to clarify the difference between the two major aspects of the masculine principle. Similarly the distinction between the yin, nurturing Feminine and the yang, assertive – inferred from the dual function of the uterus, creates a revolutionary way to look at the birthing energy of the assertive energy and to distinguish it from the phallic. This distinction is crucial—as it is hoped the present book will emphasize—to bringing about authentic change to a planet bogged down from lack of Her birthing energy, which has been systematically denigrated and avoided.

Jensen, Derrick, *A Language Older Than Words, and Endgame, Volume I, The Problem of Civilization.* In the first of these two books, using autobiographical material as a springboard, Jensen presents a cogent and shattering case for domestic violence as the prototype for the human and institutional patterns that are currently prevalent. His writing is hugely important for grasping the enormity and ubiquity of violence on the planet. The second of these works extends the first to address more explicitly the violence inherent in the relationship between urban centers and their local and remote sources of needed raw materials, and the impact this has on the environment and the health of the natural world. Both are strong medicine, but highly recommended at a time when the medicine needs to be strong to treat an illness that is severe.

Mishra, Kamalakar, *Perspectives on Tantra.* This little volume is not easily obtained, but will hopefully be republished. Dr. Mishra was brought to the US in the 1980's to teach myself and other students of Swami Rama more about Tantra. He, an humble and soft-spoken little man, had radical things to say, and many of them are found in this book, my own copy of which he gave me while he was with us. It appears to be transcripts of informal sessions of questions and answers, a format which can both suffer from digressions and sparkle with spontaneously offered gems. He is particularly engaging when he casually shoots down the shibboleths of westernized yoga, with his irreverent and yet authoritative comments, e.g., on the central position of pleasure, his insistence that yoga and bhoga (pleasure) are one and the same, and his suggestion that "burning the seeds of your karma," would be a waste, since they are meant to sprout and grow—and that is what life is for.

O'Flaherty, Wendy Doniger, *Siva, The Erotic Ascetic.* [*] This is a scholarly work that collects many of the countless stories about Shiva, showing how they relate to each other, giving endless variations of many of them, and overall dazzling with the incredible extensiveness of Indic myth. While perusing this book can do a great deal to help one grasp the nature of Shiva as he lives in the Indic consciousness, its importance to the present work is the way that it makes clear that Shiva is an image, a concept, a personage which was not able to exist within a purely Western world view: Erotic and ascetic have not been considered characteristics that can coexist in humans. It simply didn't compute. That is why the arrival of Shiva in our mythical consciousness is so revolutionary (as is that of Kali for different reasons).

Odier, Daniel, *The Yoga Spandakarika, The Sacred Texts at the Origins of Tantra.* These ancient writings carry the most authentic glimpse of what *spanda* was to the people who developed Tantra. There are many other versions and many commentaries on them, but this rendition, by a Westerner, is poetically put together and interwoven with information about Tantra teachers and traditions, and is very accessible to the reader from the West.

Rama, Swami and **Ajaya**, Swami, *The Creative Use of Emotion.* For most of us the major pitfall in tackling a sticky path such as Tantra is the emotional quick sands we can slip into. The simple, yet effective, approaches to understanding

[*]   Siva, with the mark over the S is pronounced Shiva.

your emotions and working with them described in this small volume are must haves on the trail.

Rama, Swami, *Love Whispers*. Love poems and prose pieces to the Goddess, written by my teacher.

Rama, Swami, *Path of Fire and Light, Vol 2*. Probably the most concise and comprehensive description available of the basic practices that undergird the more advanced paths of yoga and Tantra. Includes topics such as: Transforming Negative Thought Patterns, Understanding The Mind And The States Of Consciousness, Preparing Body And Breath, The Power Of Determination And Will, The Science Of Sound, Death And Transition, etc. Very useful for cutting through the morass of "yogas on the market" currently.

Rama, Swami, **Ballentine**, Rudolph, and **Hymes**, Alan, *Science of Breath, A Practical Guide*. Breath work is one of the foundations of Tantra. This little book presents the basic information needed to work successfully with the breath and the subtle energy shifts that correspond to it. Chapters on: Diaphragmatic Breathing, Nasal Function and The Nadis, and Basic Breathing Techniques. Indispensable.

Rama, Swami, **Ballentine**, Rudolph, MD, **Ajaya**, Swami, PhD, *Yoga and Psychotherapy, the Evolution of Consciousness*. This book, which was published in 1976, is still used as a text in university courses on the study of consciousness. It is particularly useful in learning your way around in the various realms of consciousness that overlay the unitary consciousness. It includes a concise and useful description of the chakras.

Saran, Prem, *Yoga, Bhoga, and Ardhanarishvara*. Saran's little volume (adapted from his doctoral dissertation), throws needed light on several important issues that surround Tantra. The most important are: gender, and how it is held in the Indic psyche; pleasure, and its major role in the culture out of which Tantra grew; and the matter of individuality, and how dramatically different it is constituted in India as compared to the West. Saran is qualified to comment on these issues, since he is not only a PhD in anthropology and a practitioner of Tantra himself, but also a straddler of cultures. He was born in Kerala, one of the historic repositories of tantric knowledge and practice, spent much of his childhood in Western Schools (later in life also spending protracted periods in the US to complete his graduate education), and married a woman from Assam, another stronghold of Tantra, and has lived most of his adult life there. He also has the fresh perspective that comes from having worked most of his life outside academia.

Shankaranarayanan, S, *The Ten Great Cosmic Powers*. This is a book about the ten *Mahavidyas*. *Maha* means "great," and *vidya* means "knowledge" or "wisdom." The ten Mahavidyas are the ten goddesses about whom, it is said, if one knows all, then one would know everything about the entire phenomenal universe. That is true because all manifestation is merely a display of Her many splendors. In other words, She is the creator of all this diverse world: "She nods and the worlds appear." It is Her taste for variety, embodiment, and sensual delight that leads to this panoply of manifestations. The "worship" of each of the ten Mahavidyas is a process of contemplating Her, finding that part of oneself that corresponds to Her nature and coming to accept and honor it. Though it is short and rather coarsely produced, this is the best book I have seen (and there are a number) describing the character of each Mahavidya and the details of the practices that corresponds to Her.

Sinha, Indra, *Tantra, The Cult of Ectasy*. This is an 81/2 x 11 inch book, which has many color illustrations and extensive text that is full of intriguing tantra lore. But I recommend it primarily for the fifteen tantric ritual paintings that are beautifully reproduced therein. Most of them full page, they are striking and of a hypnotic quality. They depict the goddess (and occasionally other deities) in ways that dramatize and clarify the extremely radical and transgressive concept of the Feminine that is so peculiar to Tantra. According to the author, the paintings, from the 18th century, were not intended to be "art," but rather objects of meditation and for use in ritual. Indeed many of them are spattered with what appears to be body fluids. Contemplation of these paintings provides a powerful non-verbal, alogical introduction to Tantra.

Svoboda, Robert. *Aghora, At the Left Hand of God*. Svoboda was the first American to complete a full degree program in Ayurveda in India. While he was there, he became the student of an Indian teacher named Vimalananda. This book is the first of three intended to convey Vimalananda's teachings. It is worth its price for the cover alone: a striking portrait of "Smashan Tara," one manifestation of Kali. It's a fearsome picture, with a Kapalika or Aghora (the variety of tantrica who tends the cremation grounds, or *smashan*, in order to perform rituals and practices with the dead) featured as well, and the story of Vimalananda's initial encounter with the goddess is one of the most memorable narratives in modern tantric literature. I often read it to groups of students to offer them a sense of the breadth of tantra practice in India.

Talbot, Michael, *The Holographic Universe*. This book describes the emerging use of the holographic model by science, with a special focus on the work of David Bohm in quantum physics and Karl Pribram in neuroscience. After establishing that the use of the holographic concept has good pedigree, he suggests its application to understanding and bringing into the fold of science a variety of otherwise inexplicable phenomena which are usually regarded as "fringe science" or are frankly discounted, such as "out of body experiences." The book is a major step toward reclaiming the vaster realms of human experience for the application of a more open minded and mature version of science. Very helpful for the reader who finds descriptions of tantra "unbelievable."

Tigunait, Rajmani, *Tantra Unveiled*. Full disclosure: Pandit Tigunait is a guru *bhai* of mine (we had the same teacher). But I am not alone in considering this small volume an excellent introduction to authentic Tantra. It covers its origins and history, current developments in India, and clears up a number of misunderstandings.

Wise, Anna, *The High Performance Mind*. For those who require hard data to back up the discussion of the "Structures of Consciousness" detailed in Gebser and described in the Mandukyopanishad, this book will fill the bill. It is one of several the author has written on her pioneering work with EEG biofeedback. With the spectrum analysis of brainwaves and immediate feedback technology, she has demonstrated (and I experienced it first hand in her lab!) that one can objectively identify the shift from Mental to Mythical, Mythical to Magic, etc. (She uses different terminology.) A unique bridge between East and West.

Rudolph Ballentine is a retired holistic physician and psychiatrist, who spends his time practicing, teaching, and writing about tantra and permaculture, living in and co-evolving an ecovillage, and stewarding a small neighborhood that is exploring the building of community on the principles of tantra as articulated in this book. He has four children whom he adores and whose engagement with the world is also a major part of his current course of study.